Deo Farrugia

# User's Motivation For Using Facebook

GRIN Publishing

**Bibliographic information published by the German National Library:**

The German National Library lists this publication in the National Bibliography; detailed bibliographic data are available on the Internet at http://dnb.dnb.de .

**Imprint:**

Copyright © 2014 GRIN Verlag GmbH
Print and binding: Books on Demand GmbH, Norderstedt Germany
ISBN: 978-3-656-95073-8

**This book at GRIN:**

http://www.grin.com/en/e-book/298721/user-s-motivation-for-using-facebook

# What motivation attracts different users to use Facebook?

**Project Report**

*Submitted in Partial Fulfilment of the*

*Requirements for the Degree of*

**Computing and Information Technology**

*to the*

**University of Derby**

*By*

| | |
|---|---|
| **Name:** | Deo Farrugia |
| **Degree:** | Bachelor of Science (Honours) in Computing and Information Technology |
| **Date:** | 19Th May 2014 |

*Abstract* - Over the last few years social network websites have become a global phenomenon and brought great social impact across the world. Such happenings deserve to be studied and their many aspects investigated thoroughly. The aim of this study was to explore the motives and preferences of users on Facebook. The data was obtained through an online survey on 383 random participants. The result confirmed that Facebook has become a powerful medium of communication. Younger people between ages 14 to 21 are the users who spend more time on Facebook and like to chat with school friends, while age 22 and up chat more with old friends and family members. A sense of security is shown across all ages, gender and education level as in the majority the participants declared that their profile can be only viewed by friends and that they have few unknown friends on Facebook.

# Acknowledgment

I would never have been able to finish my dissertation without the guidance of my tutor, help from work colleagues, and support from my wife.

I would like to express my gratitude to my tutor, Dr. Eleanor Dare, for her excellent guidance, patience, and prompt feedback throughout the research. I would like to thank my work colleagues, Conrad Dimech, Silvianne Buttigieg, and Jacqueline Cefai who helped me out carrying the survey with students. I would also to thank other work colleagues who helped me sharing the survey to other users.

Finally, I would like to thank my wife, Melanie Ruth Farrugia. She was always there cheering me up and stood by me through the good and bad times.

# Table of Contents

## List of tables

## List of Figures

# 2 Literature Review

An extensive range of papers and studies have been analysed in order to identify the most relevant research on Facebook. This literature review will enable to look and build on previous findings and studies. The importance of each citation has been based on the number of times it had been cited by the other studies.

## 2.1    Social Networks Popularity

Many different studies and reviews have been done on defining a social network. According to Farkas (2010), social networks are basically a meeting of people who share the same interests and join a community (Farkas, 2010). Boyd and Ellision define social media as:

(1)      Constructing a public or semi-public profile within a bounded system,

(2)      Articulating a list of other users with whom they share a connection,

(3)      View and traversing their list of connections and those made by others within the system. The nature and nomenclature of these connections may vary from site to site (Boyd and Ellision, 2007).

From all the social network sites available the most popular is Facebook (Hew, 2011). Researches show that anywhere between 85 and 99% of college students use Facebook (Hargittai, 2007), (Matney and Borland, 2009).

## 2.2    Motivation to use Facebook

Facebook started in 2004 as a social network at Harvard University (Cassidy, 2006). Facebook allows users to create a personal 'profile' which includes user details such as name, surname, age, marital status and general information like education background, work background, and favourite interests. Other details that can be linked to the profile include pictures and videos such as song clips. Facebook also allows interaction between users such that it permits users to post messages on other users' pages, post and tag pictures and videos, among other things (Zywica and Danowski, 2008).

Studies on Facebook users' activity show that the most popular reason to use Facebook is that they like to keep in touch with other people and to know them better (Joinson, 2008), (Golder, Wilkinson and Huberman, 2007), (Sheldon, 2008), (Farrugia and Wiese, 2009). An interesting survey that can help us build our report was carried out by Stern and Taylor (2007) on 364 university students, and found out that very few students tried to meet new people or tried to initiate a relationship through Facebook, but most of them tend to maintain already existing relationships (Stern and Taylor, 2007).

A common agreement between different studies confirms that Facebook is frequently used to maintain distant relationships, as this allows direct communication between users who are apart from each other (Urista, Dong and Day, 2008) (Golder, Wilkinson and Huberman, 2007) (Sheldon, 2008). The study by Bryant and Marmo (2012) shows the behaviour of relationships that a group of college students had with their Facebook friends (Bryant and Marmo, 2012) . The study shows that relationships on Facebook are casual relationships or already known friends. Furthermore, the study reveals that couples and close friends tend to use other means to maintain their relationships. According to the users interviewed, they do not consider Facebook to allow sufficient intimacy for maintaining close relationships. They consider the communication over Facebook as 'cheap' and not adequate enough to maintain serious relationships with people, unless geographically distant. Stern and Taylor (2007) have obtained the same results, that is, students mostly use Facebook to keep in touch with friends and develop relationships. Moreover, the study shows that it is not used for romantic relationships development. When analysing these findings, it is assumed that students do not want their dating attempts to be in some way public (Stern and Taylor, 2007).

A deep and more complex opinion is a report from Boyd and Ellison (2007) which says that most research on social network sites is more concentrated on impression management and friendship performance, networks and network structure, online/offline connections, and privacy issues. This could be a gap in our literature review when trying to find why Facebook has become so popular. Our report will try to address this gap by measuring Facebook or what people think the reason is for Facebook to have become so popular.


2.3    Social Media differences, Different Age Groups and Education levels


DeBell and Chapman's (2006) report showed that computers and internet are most popular within the adolescents and young adults age band (DeBell and Chapman, 2006). Social network websites have become a popular online communication tool that allows users to create a public or private profile to interact with people in their networks (Boyd & Ellison, 2008).

A study conducted by Poellhuber, Normand and Anderson (2011) intended to find the use of and interest in social media. This report will help us categorize our interviewers' age bands. An online questionnaire which consisted of 90 questions, was completed by 3,462 students between July, 2009 and February, 2010. A large percentage of females (75.3%), responded to the survey. The respondents to the survey where categorized according to age. Each age category was given a name as shown in table 1.

Table 1: Different category represented in the study conducted Pollhuber, Normand and Anderson. (**Poellhuber, Roy and Anderson, 2011**).

| Age | Name |
|---|---|
| 16-24 | Generation Z |
| 25-32 | Generation Y |
| 33-40 | Generation X2 |
| 41-48 | Generation X1 |
| 49 and over | Baby boomers |

In terms of user proficiency, the results revealed that a significant percentage, around 69.5% of the survey respondents, reported being either advanced or expert users of social networking. In video sharing the results show 52.9%, 33.7% in photo sharing and 25.4% in blogging. The significant difference that can be seen from the study done by Poellhuber, Normand and Anderson (2011) in social media usage, reveals that younger people aged 16 to 32 of different genders, tend to be, or say they are "self-professed experts" in comparison to adults of a more advanced age (Poellhuber, Roy and Anderson, 2011). Turkle (2011) in her book showed how adolescents can show their real feelings on Facebook rather than real life. Young people tend to worry that their profile appearance might not be so interesting to others and participants describe as Facebook as a tearful place for them (Turkle, 2011). Pempek, Yermolayeva and Calvert study shows that through the use of social media, college students are able to disclose information about themselves and then receive feedback on it from their peers (Pempek, Yermolayeva and Calvert, 2009).

Another study was carried out between November 12 and December 2012 by Duggan and Brenner (2013) among 1,802 respondents who are internet users. The study revealed that 67% of the respondents use a type of social network website and confirms the popularity of Facebook in all categories (age, gender and education level). The study categorises the education level in three levels which are high school graduate, attended some college and others that have some college qualification. (Duggan and Brenner, 2013).

Arnold and Paulus' (2010) research in the educational field proposed that numerous educational information is being shared on social networks. However, the report points out that there can be misuse in sharing as well and highlighted that teachers do not have direct control over misused sharing. It also points out that there must be prevention on such kind of sharing (Arnold and Paulus, 2010). With these grounds of other studies, our report could be used to point out possible improvements that can be done to Facebook in the educational sector.

## 2.4    Social Networks Trend Differences between Genders

A study by Bonds-Raacke and Raacke (2010), shows that there are no big differences between men and women in social networking usage. The most popular use for social networking sites for both genders is to keep in touch with old friends. From the study some differences emerged between men and women usage in social networking. Men use social networking to share information about themselves and used the site for dating purposes more when compared to women. On the other hand, women tend to set more privacy settings to their profile account. The study showed that men have significantly more friends linked to their profiles than women. (Bonds-Raacke and Raacke, 2010).

A general consensus from current studies shows that the most common reasons why people use social networks is to keep in touch with friends, making new friends, share photos and join groups with whom they share the same interest. This can help us relate to our studies and suggest improvements on our study. This study should help us identify usage of Facebook within different age groups. It will also help determine whether students are wasting time on Facebook or somehow benefit from it for their education.

# 3    Methodology

## 3.1    Main objectives

- Any particular habit difference between people of a different age?
- Does usage differ between different education levels?
- Any difference in how the two genders relate to Facebook usage?

## 3.2    Hypothesis

In addition to the proposed research survey, the following hypothesis will be used to conclude different aspects of the study:

H1: Different aged participants will have different trends on using Facebook.

H2: Young age users will be more active on Facebook.

## 3.3    Type of Study

Several study methods of research were analysed before a decision was taken. The decision taken was to use a study based on quantitative research. These type of researches focus on capturing data through means of a questioner.  Questioners are a valuable method to collect representative data. An efficacious quantitative research requires a large sample of data and that it is a representative sample of the required target market.

## 3.4    Questioner design

The questioner was designed on the main objectives as specified above. The questioner consists of 14 questions which mainly focus on the usage of Facebook. This will help us determine preferences or differences which may exist between different genders, ages and education levels. A pilot study was conducted to check the validity of the questioner. This was done by asking different people to take the survey and collect their feedback. From the feedback collected some of the questions were improved to allow easy understanding of the questions.

## 3.5    Sample selection

From previous studies research it emerged that most studies were conducted on ages from 18 years up. This limited studies only to 'Adults' groups and missing information from 'Young' group range. To ensure the quality of information, a proportion to various ages and gender categories will be used. In Malta, this research will be conducted on around 217,040 users subscribed to Facebook (Miniwatts Marketing Group, 2013). Additional demographics data regarding Facebook users will be represented in this study. Socialbakers (2014) shows that 52% are male and 48% Female users. When it comes to age, the largest age group is 25-34 followed by age group 18-24 (Socialbakers, 2014). A sample of 383 respondents was selected with confidence interval of 95% and 5% confidence interval. Hence the result will vary approximately by ±5%.

## 3.6    Data collection

Marketing to reply for this questioner was conducted over Secondary schools, post-Secondary College, tertiary institutions, popular Facebook groups and word of mouth. The informants will be asked around 17 questions. Through such, informants will provide their Facebook preferences, experiences and motivation. Questions range from demographic information to more intuitive questions, such as what they use Facebook for. After data collection, data cleaning was performed to ensure that results are consistent and categorical variables are well categorized to ensure efficiency of results.

## 3.7 Statistical Analysis

Planning the statistical analysis is an integral part of planning a questioner. The survey outcome will show us some means or proportion affected of different groups such as age group to the time spent on Facebook. The aim of the statistical analysis is to explore and presenting large amounts of data to determine underlying patterns and trends. To get an accurate results in our statistical analysis both Microsoft Excel and SPSS Statistics software are used.

In our Statistical analysis we are using the Chi-Square statistic which compares observed data against expected data based on a specific hypothesis. Chi square ($\chi^2$) statistic is used to examine if distributions of categorical variables contrast from one another. The categorical variables produce data in the categories and numerical variables produce numerical form data. The Chi square statistics compares the totals of categories responses with two or more groups.

The Chi-Square statistic formula is

$$\chi^2 = \sum_{i=1}^{n} \frac{(\text{Observed}_i - \text{Expected}_i)^2}{\text{Expected}_i}$$

Other analysis to our data is the Analysis of Variance (ANOVA) which is used to test the significant differences in means when considering 3 or more samples, and cannot be done with a standard t-test that compares two samples at a time. To apply Analysis of Variance, the tests use the F-statistics which compares the 'Variation' within the sample is given by:

$$f = \frac{Mean\ Square\ Between\ samples}{Mean\ Square\ Within\ sample}$$

# 4 Data Analysis

## 4.1 Demographics

The variables in this research study consisted of three demographic characteristics, which are age, gender and education level. The number and percentage of the participants in each demographic characteristic are presented below.

*Age*

The major participants (35.25%, n=135) are aged between 14 and 17 years old. The second category of participants (29.24, n= 112) who respond to the questioner are the aged 18 to 21 years old. 93 Participants were 22 to 34 years old and only 43 were over 35 years of age.

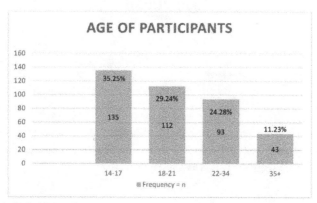

Figure 1: Age distribution of sample.

When comparing the above statistics with the actual age distribution of Facebook users as cited from, Socialbakers (2014), there is some age bias. During the following analysis this will be accounted for and hence wherever is the need a special attention will be put in the interpretation of results.

*Gender*

The distribution between males (51.44%, n=197) and females (48.56%, n=186) is representative of the actual age distribution of the populations as cited from Socialbakers (2014).

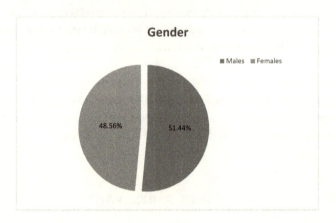

Figure 2: Gender distribution of the sample.

*Education level*

The majority of the participants were post-secondary level (48.2%, n=184) followed by secondary school level (30.1%, n= 115). The tertiary education level came in third (18.3%, n=70) and last vocational level (3.45%, n=13).

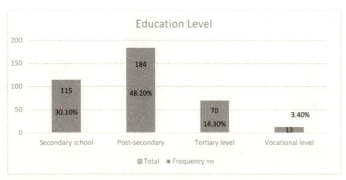

Figure 3: Education level of participants.

## 4.2 Descriptive statistic

The survey results show that the majority (93.9%) of the participants have been using Facebook more than a year as shown in table 3–Appendix A-1. In most questions in this section there might be some bias as older users tend to have slightly different answers when compared with younger users. All results will be analysed in further details in the next section.

In table 2–Appendix A-1 we can see that the majority of the participants (28.2%, n=107) said, that they update their Facebook status monthly followed by those who update their status weekly (26.1%, n=99). A substantial amount of 20.3%, n= 77 says that they never update their status.

An interesting outcome from table 4–Appendix A-1 is that the majority of participants (63.5%, n= 242) update their profile picture few times a week. Around 25.9% update their profile picture few times a month. Still there is quite few participants (7.4%, n= 29) that never update their profile picture. Moreover, almost all participants are in some Facebook groups as shown in table 5–Appendix A-1. As shown in table 7–Appendix A-1 participants' majority (84.2%, n= 319) use Facebook on different devices.

Facebook's popularity as a means of communication can be seen in table 8–Appendix A-1. The majority of participants (66.1%, n=251) say that they prefer to communicate with friends using Facebook. The second place method of communication is the use of Telephone (21.6%, n=82) and the third placed method is Skype (8.4%, n=32). Email method is the least preferred method.

From table 10–AppendixA-1, one concludes that the majority of Facebook users allow only their friends to view their profile (68.7%, n= 259). This can be interpreted as users are aware of security implications.

## 4.3 Comparative Analysis

When comparing age group against the 'How long have you been signed up on Facebook?' question, Chi-squared test found that there is a statistical significant different with a p-value of less than 0.05 (p-value = 0.045). Mainly this difference is coming due to the age group 35+, since 14.3% of respondents claimed that their registration to Facebook is 'months' old while for the other age groups only 5.3% or less selected the same option. When comparing the same question with gender, Chi-squared test found no significant difference (p-value = 0.339) between gender and age of Facebook's users account. On the other hand, there is an association (p-value = 0.038) when comparing education level and age of Facebook's users account. In fact those that are up to 'vocational' level of education are less likely to have registered on Facebook for a longer period.

The comparison between the age group against the 'How often do you update your profile?' shows a significant difference in the age group 35+, as 32.6% of the respondents stated that they never update their profile picture whereas other age groups only 6.5% and less selected the same option. When comparing gender to the same question there was a high difference between the gender and photo profile update. While male gender declared that 73.6% update their profile few times a year, the female participants declared that 52.4 % update their profile monthly. Comparing the same question with education level, showed that significant differences exist, as around 71% from the post-secondary level and tertiary level of education participants declared that they update their profile picture monthly while only 45.6% of Secondary level of education participants update their profile monthly.

In table 24–Appendix A-2 the age is compared with 'How many groups have you joined on Facebook' shows that there is significant difference between different age groups (p-value =

12

0.00). The younger generation tend to join more Facebook groups when compared with the older generation. Moreover, around 15% of those 35 years or more are not in any Facebook group, while those of a younger age, almost all of them are in at least one group. On the contrary when comparing the gender to the question 'How many groups have joined on Facebook' showed that there are no major differences between genders (p-value=0.09). Again the education level factor has shown no major differences when participants were asked how many groups have they joined.

When participants were asked what applications they prefer to use on Facebook, results show that games are the most popular applications by all participants. The age factor showed no difference at all in all applications (games, music and videos). On the other hand the gender has shown that the majority of female respondents like to play games on Facebook (51.6%) whiles the males' majority do not prefer to play games (70.6%). Chi-squared test found that there is a statistical significant difference with a p-value of less than 0.05 (p-value = 0.000).There were no major differences when comparing males and females to music applications usage. However when comparing the video application 33% from the males respondents to the females, males prefer the video application while only 18% of females prefer this application. In fact a statistical significant difference was found for this comparison. The Education level showed no major differences between the applications although the vocational education level showed low results in all applications.

In table 48–Appendix A-2, when comparing age with the question 'Do you use Facebook on different Devices?', chi-squared test found a statistical significant difference (p-value = 0.000). The age group 14-17 showed that the majority (88.6%) used Facebook on other devices. The least age group that use Facebook on other devices are the 35+ of age (65.1%). No major differences is shown when comparing gender against whether they use Facebook on different devices. On the other hand, a significant difference exists when comparing different education levels with the same question. Vocational participants (61.5%) tend to use less other gaming devices when compared with secondary (82.5%), post-secondary (88.4%) and tertiary level of education (80%).

When comparing participants' age with 'how they prefer to communicate with friends' chi-squared test found an association between the two variables. 15.7% of those at younger age (14-17) use the phone to communication with friends, and for the same age group 15.7% use Skype. On the hand for the older age groups higher number of people use phone and less number of people use Skype. Those of younger generation (21 and less) tend to use more Facebook (66-72%) when compared with those of 22 years and over (around 61%). When comparing the same question with gender and education, chi-squared test found significant association between these variables. Males tend to use more Skype (12.2% vs 4.3%) and Facebook (69.9% vs 62%) than females, while females (28.3%) tend to use more phones than males (15.3%). Secondary level of education users (16.5%) tend to use more Skype when compared with other levels of education (7.7% and less). Tertiary level of education students use their e-mail (8.8%) and phone (26.5%) more than any other group.

Participants where specifically asked what type of friends they have on their Facebook account. When comparing participants' age with 'Type of friends School Friends' chi-square test showed a statistical difference (p–value=0.000). The age group 14-17 showed majority (70.7%) followed by the age group 18 to 21 at 70.6 %. The group that have least school friends are the age group 35 + at 35.5%. All ages show that they have few "Friends you actually never met". There is no significant difference as shown from Chi-square test where the p-value = .301. The majority that have least never met friends are the age group 35+ at 56.6% which could be an indication of a more mature approach to security. When asked about family members there is a significant difference between ages (p-values = .001). The age group 35+ show majority (60%) that agree that they have family members as friends. The age group 14-17 at 21.7% show that they do not have family members as friends. When comparing age to old friends the chi square test show that there is no major significant difference between ages (p-value=.006). Again when asking if they have foreign friends as Facebook friends there are no significant differences between ages (p-value= .090). The same questions are compared against the gender and showed that there are no major differences when asked if they have school friends (p-value=.972). When asked both genders if they have family members as friends, the chi-square test showed a significant difference between gender (p-value=.000). Female gender showed that they have more family members as friends (45.8%) than males (23.2%). When both genders are compared with old friends as Facebook friends there is a significant difference (p-value=.001). Females declare that they have more old friends (36.7%). When asked for foreign friends both genders showed no significant difference (p-value= 0.063).

All questions were compared again to the education level and showed that there is a significant difference (p-value =.002) as post –secondary education majority (68.2%) agree to have more school friends followed by Secondary school level (56.6%). This could be a biased indication as both are still attending school. There is no significant difference (p-value=0.679) with all levels of education when asked if they have never met friends as Facebook friends. There are no significant difference when comparing family members (p-value=0.155), old friends (p-value=0.038) and foreign friends (p-value=0.529). Friends never actually met (p-value=.133).

The last questions compare actual preferences participants have on Facebook. Age group 14-17 majority (77.7%) declare that they use Facebook to communicate with Friends. Age group 35+ majority (55.6%) declared that they use Facebook to communicate with Family members. The age group 35+ majority (45.5%) also declared the use Facebook to communicate with old friends. There were no major differences between all ages when asked if they use Facebook to communicate with friends out of the country (p-value=0.019).When participants were asked if they use Facebook to play games, age group 35+ majority (52.6%) agreed with statement followed by age group 22-34 (26.3%). All age groups show same level of response when asked if they use Facebook to share photos or videos (p-value=0.451).There were no major differences between genders when compared what they use Facebook for. Again there were no major differences when comparing Facebook preferences to the education level as Chi-square for all statement returned a p-value greater than 0.005.

# 5    Conclusion

Over the last years social network websites have become very popular and have attracted many users but at the same also created a lot of criticism. This study pushed analysis a step forward as why people use Facebook and why they tend to spend time on it. The research proposed some hypothesis and questions to examine the relationship between motivations for using Facebook and user preferences.

The above results show that Facebook is most popular method of communication over all other communication mediums across all ages, gender and education level. The research showed and ruled out the second hypothesis, that 'younger' people aged 14 to 21 are more active on Facebook than 'older' people aged 21 and over.

More females are inclined to play games while more men are inclined to share videos on Facebook. Female participants declared that they have more family members as friends compared to men.

This research shows that there is a sense of awareness of security as the majority of participants declared that they have few "never met friends" on their friend list although results show that older users (21+) are more aware of the required security. When participants were asked who can see their profiles all age groups declared that "only friends" can see their profile. Younger age persons (age 14 to 21) have more school friends while older age (22+) have more old friends and family members.

The study showed that almost all participants have joined Facebook groups. This could be an indication that users on Facebook have a sense of belonging with other people, due to same preferences and common interests. This research was limited to how much groups participants have joined, future research may investigate why participants joined the groups.

As a recommendation for future research, motivation of those who do not use Facebook could be analysed for comparison. While this research was targeted to Facebook users in Malta using an online questioner, other studies can be performed using telephone and/or face to face interviews to reach a wider target of people.

# References

Arnold, N. and Paulus, T. (2010) 'Using a social networking site for experiential learning', *The Internet and Higher Education*, vol. 13, no. 4, pp. 188-196.

Bonds-Raacke, J. and Raacke, J. (2010) 'MySpace and Facebook: Identifying Dimensions of Uses and Gratifications for Friend Networking Sites', *Individual Differences Research*, vol. 11, no. 2, pp. 27-33.

Bosch, T.E. (2009) 'Using online social networking for teaching and learning: Facebook use at the University of Cape Town', *South African Journal for Communication Theory and Research*, vol. 35, no. 2, pp. 185-200.

Boyd, D.M. and Ellision, N.B. (2007) 'Social Network Sites: Definition, History, and Scholarship', *Journal of Computer-Mediated Communciation*, vol. 13, no. 1, pp. 210-230.

Bryant, E. and Marmo, J. (2012) 'Relational Maintenance Strategies on Facebook: A two-stage examination of interaction rules in close, casual, and acquaintance friendships', *Journal of Social and Personal Relationships*, vol. 29, no. 8, pp. 1013-1035.

Cassidy, J. (2006) *ME MEDIA - How hanging out on the Internet became big business.*, 15 May, [Online], Available: http://www.newyorker.com/archive/2006/05/15/060515fa_fact_cassidy [23 November 2013].

DeBell, M. and Chapman, C. (2006) *Computer and Internet Use by Students in 2003*, Washington: U.S. Department of Education.

Duggan, M. and Brenner, J. (2013) *The Demographics of Social Media Users*, Washington: Pew Research Center's Internet & American Life Project.

Farkas, P.A. (2010) *Senior Social Platform – An application aimed to reduce the social and digital isolation of seniors*, [Online], Available: http://www.corp.at/archive/CORP2010_223.pdf [21 November 2013].

Farrugia, R. and Wiese, D. (2009) 'Coordinating communication on Facebook: An analysis of meaning development through close relationships', Paper presented at the annual meeting of the NCA 95th Annual Convention, Chicago Hilton & Towers, Chicago IL.

Golder, S., Wilkinson, D. and Huberman, B. (2007) 'Rhythms of social interaction: messaging within a massive online', *3rd International Conference on Communities and Technologies*.

Hargittai, E. (2007) 'Whose space? Differences among users and non-users of social network site', *Computer-Mediated Communication*, vol. 13, no. 1, pp. 276–297.

Hew, K.F. (2011) 'Students' and teachers' use of Facebook', *Computers in Human* , vol. 27, no. 2, pp. 662-676.

Joinson, A.N. (2008) '"Looking at, "Looking up' or "Keeping up with People? Motivation and use of facebook', *Proceedings of the SIGCHI Conference on Human Factors in Computing Systems*, pp. 1027-1036.

Matney, M. and Borland, K. (2009) *Facebook, blogs, tweets: How staff and units can use social networking to enhance student learning*, [Online], Available: http://studentlife.umich.edu/research/files/research/FacebookforNASPA6Mar09.pdf [20 November 2013].

Miniwatts Marketing Group (2013) *Internet World Stats Usage and Population Statistics*, [Online], Available: http://www.internetworldstats.com/europa.htm [10 Febuary 2014].

Pempek, T.A., Yermolayeva, Y.A. and Calvert, S.L. (2009) 'College students' social networking experiences on Facebook', *Journal of Applied Developmental Psychology*, vol. 30, no. 3, pp. 227-238.

Poellhuber, B., Roy, N. and Anderson, T. (2011) 'Distance Students' Readiness for Social Media and Collaboration', *The International Review of Research in Open and Distance Learning*, vol. 12, no. 6.

Sheldon, P. (2008) 'The relationship between unwillingness-to-communicate and students' Facebook use', *Journal of Media Psychology: Theories, Methods, and Applications*, vol. 20, no. 2, pp. 67-75.

Socialbakers (2014) *Socialbakers*, [Online], Available: http://www.socialbakers.com/facebook-statistics/malta [10 Febuary 2014].

Stern, L.A. and Taylor, k. (2007) 'Social Networking on Facebook', *Journal of the Communication, Speech & Theatre Association of North Dakota*, vol. 20, pp. 9-20.

Stutzman, F. (2006) *Student life on the Facebook*, January, [Online], Available: http://www.ibiblio.org/fred/facebook/stutzman_fbook.pdf [16 January 2013].

Turkle, S. (2011) *Alone Together: Why We Expect More from Technology and Less from Each Other*, New York: Basic Books.

Urista, M.A., Dong, Q. and Day, K.D. (2008) 'Explaining Why Young Adults Use MySpace and Facebook', *Human Communication. A Publication of the Pacific and Asian Communication Association*, vol. 12, no. 2, pp. 215-229.

Zywica, J. and Danowski, J. (2008) 'The Faces of Facebookers: Investigating Social Enhancement and Social Compensation Hypotheses; Predicting FacebookTM and Offline

Popularity from Sociability and Self-Esteem, and Mapping the Meanings of Popularity with Semantic Networks', *Journal of Computer-Mediated Communication*, vol. 14, no. 1, pp. 1-34.

# Appendix A-1

## Descriptive statistics

Table 2: You're Facebook 'status' update?

|        |                    | Frequency n | Valid Percentage | Cumulative Percentage |
|--------|--------------------|-----------|------------------|-----------------------|
| Valid  | A few times a day  | 51        | 13.5%            | 13.5%                 |
|        | A few times a week | 99        | 26.1%            | 39.6%                 |
|        | A few times a month| 107       | 28.2%            | 67.8%                 |
|        | A few times a year | 45        | 11.9%            | 79.7%                 |
|        | Never              | 77        | 20.3%            | 100.0%                |
|        | Total              | 379       | 100.0%           |                       |
| Missing| System             | 4         |                  |                       |
|        | Total              | 383       |                  |                       |

Table 3: How long have you been signed up to Facebook.

|        |        | Frequency N | Valid Percentage | Cumulative Percentage |
|--------|--------|-----------|------------------|-----------------------|
| Valid  | Weeks  | 4         | 1.1%             | 1.1%                  |
|        | Months | 19        | 5.0%             | 6.1%                  |
|        | Years  | 357       | 93.9%            | 100%                  |
|        | Total  | 380       | 100%             |                       |
| Missing| System | 3         |                  |                       |
| Total  |        | 383       |                  |                       |

Table 4: How often update profile picture.

|  |  | Frequency n | Valid Percentage | Cumulative Percentage |
|---|---|---|---|---|
| Valid | A few times a day | 3 | .8% | .8% |
|  | A few times a week | 9 | 2.4% | 3.1% |
|  | A few times a month | 99 | 25.9% | 29.1% |
|  | A few times a year | 242 | 63.4% | 92.4% |
|  | Never | 29 | 7.4% | 100.0% |
|  | Total | 382 | 100.0% |  |
| Missing | System | 1 |  |  |
|  | Total | 383 |  |  |

Table 5: How many "Groups" have you joined on Facebook?

|  |  | Frequency n | Valid Percentage | Cumulative Percentage |
|---|---|---|---|---|
| Valid | 1-10 | 165 | 43.7% | 43.7% |
|  | 11-20 | 131 | 34.7% | 78.3% |
|  | 21 or more | 71 | 18.8% | 97.1% |
|  | None | 11 | 2.9% | 100% |
|  | Total | 378 | 100.0 |  |
| Missing | System | 5 |  |  |
|  | Total | 383 |  |  |

Table 6: More than one Facebook account?

|  |  | Frequency N | Valid Percentage | Cumulative Percentage |
|---|---|---|---|---|
| Valid | Yes | 45 | 11.9% | 11.9% |
|  | No | 334 | 88.1% | 100% |
|  | Total | 379 | 100% |  |
| Missing | System | 4 |  |  |
|  | Total | 383 |  |  |

Table 7: Do you use Facebook on different devices?

|        |        | Frequency N | Valid Percentage | Cumulative Percentage |
|--------|--------|-----------|------------------|------------------------|
| Valid  | Yes    | 319       | 84.2%            | 84.2%                  |
|        | No     | 60        | 15.8%            | 100%                   |
|        | Total  | 379       | 100%             |                        |
| Missing | System | 4        |                  |                        |
|        | Total  | 383       |                  |                        |

Table 8: Preferred method to communicate with friends.

|        |          | Frequency N | Valid Percentage | Cumulative Percentage |
|--------|----------|-----------|------------------|------------------------|
| Valid  | Email    | 15        | 3.9%             | 3.9%                   |
|        | Facebook | 251       | 66.1%            | 70%                    |
|        | Phone    | 82        | 21.6%            | 91.6%                  |
|        | Skype    | 32        | 8.4%             | 100%                   |
|        | Total    | 380       | 100%             |                        |
| Missing | System  | 3         |                  |                        |
|        | Total    | 383       |                  |                        |

Table 9: Type of friends you have on your Facebook account?

|        |                              | Frequency n | Mean | Std. Deviation |
|--------|------------------------------|-----------|------|----------------|
| Valid  | School Friends               | 357       | 4.27 | 1.086          |
|        | Friends you actually never met | 268     | 2.20 | 1.342          |
|        | Family members               | 343       | 3.36 | 1.476          |
|        | Old Friends                  | 347       | 3.55 | 1.178          |
|        | Foreign friends              | 296       | 2.38 | 1.352          |
| Valid  | N                            | 227       |      |                |

Table 10: who can see your profile?

|  |  | Frequency | Valid Percentage | Cumulative Percentage |
|---|---|---|---|---|
| Valid | Everyone | 47 | 12.5% | 12.5% |
|  | Friends of friends | 71 | 18.8% | 31.3% |
|  | Only friends | 259 | 68.7% | 100% |
|  | Total | 377 | 100% |  |
| Missing | System | 6 |  |  |
|  | Total | 383 |  |  |

Table 11: what do you typical use Facebook for?

|  | Frequency | Mean | Std. Deviation |
|---|---|---|---|
| Valid |  |  |  |
| To communicate with friends | 354 | 4.51 | .885 |
| To communicate with family members | 291 | 2.68 | 1.524 |
| To communicate with old friends | 313 | 2.82 | 1.416 |
| Communicate with friends out of the country | 258 | 2.53 | 1.447 |
| Play games | 198 | 2.38 | 1.552 |
| Share photos or videos | 286 | 3.01 | 1.366 |
| Valid  N | 156 |  |  |

# Appendix A-2

## Comparison of questions to Age, Gender and Education

Question 5

How long have you been signed up on Facebook?

Table 12: Comparing Age with question "How long have you been signed up on Facebook?"

| What is your age? | How long have you been signed up on Facebook? | | | Total |
|---|---|---|---|---|
| | Weeks | Months | Years | |
| 14-17 | 1 .8% | 7 5.3% | 125 94.0% | 133 100% |
| 18-21 | 0 .0% | 4 3.6% | 108 96.4% | 112 100% |
| 22-34 | 2 2.2% | 2 2.2% | 89 95.7% | 93 100% |
| 35+ | 1 2.4% | 6 14.3% | 35 83.3% | 42 100% |
| Total | 4 1.1% | 19 5.0% | 357 93.9% | 380 100% |

Table 13: Chi-Square test for age compared to "how long have you been signed to Facebook".

| | Value | Degree of Freedom (df) | Assumption |
|---|---|---|---|
| Pearson Chi-Square | 12.898 | 6 | .045 |
| Likelihood Ratio | 11.693 | 6 | .069 |
| Linear-by-Linear Association | 2.872 | 1 | .090 |
| No. of valid Cases | 380 | | |

Table 14: Comparing gender with question "How long have you been signed up on Facebook?"

| What is your gender? | How long have you been signed up on Facebook? | | | Total |
|---|---|---|---|---|
| | Weeks | Months | Years | |
| Males | 1 .5% | 12 6.1% | 183 93.4% | 196 100% |
| Females | 3 1.6% | 7 3.8% | 174 94.6% | 184 100% |
| Total | 4 1.1% | 19 5.0% | 357 93.9% | 380 100% |

Table 15 Chi-Square test compare gender with question "how long have you been signed to Facebook?"

| | Value | Degree of Freedom (df) | Assumption |
|---|---|---|---|
| Pearson Chi-Square | 2.166 | 2 | .339 |
| Likelihood Ratio | 2.226 | 2 | .329 |
| Linear-by-Linear Association | .001 | 1 | .980 |
| No. of valid Cases | 380 | | |

Table 16: Comparing the Education level with question "How long have you been signed up on Facebook?"

| Education Level? | How long have you been signed up on Facebook? | | | Total |
|---|---|---|---|---|
| | Weeks | Months | Years | |
| Secondary School | 4 3.6% | 6 5.4% | 102 91.1% | 112 100% |
| Post-Secondary | 0 .0% | 9 4.9% | 175 95.1% | 184 100% |
| Tertiary Education | 0 .0% | 2 2.9% | 68 97.1% | 70 100% |
| Vocational | 0 .0% | 2 15.4% | 11 84.6% | 13 100% |
| Total | 4 1.1% | 19 5.0% | 356 93.9% | 379 100% |

Table 17: Chi-Square test when comparing education level to the question "How long have you been signed to Facebook?"

| | Value | Degree of Freedom (df) | Assumption |
|---|---|---|---|
| Pearson Chi-Square | 13.328 | 6 | .038 |
| Likelihood Ratio | 12.668 | 6 | .049 |
| Linear-by-Linear Association | 2.305 | 1 | .129 |
| No. of valid Cases | 379 | | |

Question 6

How often Update profile picture?

Table 18: Compare age with how much participants update their profile picture.

| What is your age? | How often you update your profile picture? | | | | | Total |
|---|---|---|---|---|---|---|
| | A few times a day | A few times a week | A few times a month | A few times a year | Never | |
| 14-17 | 2 | 2 | 45 | 82 | 3 | 134 |
| | 1.5% | 1.5% | 33.6% | 61.2% | 2.2% | 100% |
| 18-21 | 1 | 2 | 23 | 80 | 6 | 112 |
| | .9% | 1.8% | 20.5% | 71.4% | 5.4% | 100% |
| 22-34 | 0 | 4 | 28 | 55 | 6 | 93 |
| | .0% | 4.3% | 30.1% | 59.1% | 6.5% | 100% |
| 35+ | 0 | 1 | 3 | 25 | 14 | 43 |
| | .0% | 2.3% | 7.0% | 58.1% | 32.6% | 100% |
| Total | 3 | 9 | 99 | 242 | 29 | 382 |
| | .8% | 2.4% | 25.9% | 63.4% | 7.6% | 100% |

Table 19: Chi-Square test when compare age to how much participants update their profile picture.

|  | Value | Degree of Freedom (df) | Assumption |
|---|---|---|---|
| Pearson Chi-Square | 57.838 | 12 | .000 |
| Likelihood Ratio | 46.785 | 12 | .000 |
| Linear-by-Linear Association | 15.384 | 1 | .000 |
| No. of valid Cases | 382 |  |  |

Table 20: Compare the participants' gender with how much often they update their profile picture?

| What is your gender? | How often you update your profile picture? | | | | | Total |
|---|---|---|---|---|---|---|
|  | A few times a day | A few times a week | A few times a month | A few times a year | Never |  |
| Males | 1 .5% | 2 1.0% | 38 19.3% | 145 73.6% | 11 5.6% | 197 100% |
| Females | 2 1.6% | 7 3.8% | 61 33.0% | 97 52.4% | 18 9.7% | 185 100% |
| Total | 3 .8% | 9 2.4% | 99 25.9% | 242 63.4% | 29 7.6% | 382 100% |

Table 21: Chi-Square test when comparing gender to how much often they update their profile picture.

|  | Value | Degree of freedom (df) | Assumption |
|---|---|---|---|
| Pearson Chi-Square | 19.307 | 4 | .001 |
| Likelihood Ratio | 19.588 | 4 | .001 |
| Linear-by-Linear Association | 6.163 | 1 | .013 |
| No. of valid Cases | 382 |  |  |

Table 22: Compare the participants' education level with how much participants update their profile

| Education Level | How often you update your profile picture? | | | | | Total |
|---|---|---|---|---|---|---|
| | A few times a day | A few times a week | A few times a month | A few times a year | Never | |
| Secondary School | 2 1.8% | 6 5.3% | 43 37.7% | 52 45.6% | 11 9.6% | 114 100% |
| Post-Secondary | 0 .0% | 3 1.6% | 40 21.7% | 132 71.7% | 9 4.9% | 184 100% |
| Tertiary Education | 1 1.4% | 0 0% | 14 20.0% | 49 70.0% | 6 8.6% | 70 100% |
| Vocational | 0 .0% | 0 0% | 2 15.4% | 8 61.5% | 3 23.1% | 13 100% |
| Total | 3 .8% | 9 2.4% | 99 26.0% | 241 63.3% | 29 7.6% | 381 100% |

Table 23: Chi-Square Test when comparing education level to how much participants update their profile.

| | Value | Degree of freedom (df) | Assumption |
|---|---|---|---|
| Pearson Chi-Square | 33.347 | 12 | .001 |
| Likelihood Ratio | 34.195 | 12 | .001 |
| Linear-by-Linear Association | 12.887 | 1 | .000 |
| No. of valid Cases | 381 | | |

Question 7

How many "Groups" have you joined on Facebook?

Table 24: Age compared with question "How much groups have you joined on Facebook?"

| What is your age? | How many "groups" have you joined on Facebook? | | | | Total |
|---|---|---|---|---|---|
| | 1-10 | 11-20 | 21 or more | None | |
| 14-17 | 58 | 55 | 19 | 2 | 134 |
| | 43.3% | 41.0% | 14.2% | 1.5% | 100% |
| 18-21 | 46 | 41 | 25 | 0 | 112 |
| | 41.1% | 36.3% | 22.3% | .0% | 100% |
| 22-34 | 41 | 25 | 23 | 3 | 92 |
| | 44.6% | 27.2% | 25.0% | 3.3% | 100% |
| 35+ | 20 | 10 | 4 | 6 | 40 |
| | 50.0% | 25.0% | 10.0% | 15.0% | 100% |
| Total | 165 | 131 | 71 | 11 | 378 |
| | 43.7% | 34.7% | 18.8% | 2.9% | 100% |

Table 25: Chi-Square test when compare age to the question "how much groups have you joined on Facebook?"

| | Value | Degree of freedom (df) | Assumption |
|---|---|---|---|
| Pearson Chi-Square | 34.935 | 9 | .000 |
| Likelihood Ratio | 28.702 | 9 | .001 |
| Linear-by-Linear Association | 1.832 | 1 | .176 |
| No. of valid Cases | 378 | | |

Table 26: Gender compared to question "How much groups have you joined on Facebook?

| What is your Gender? | How many "groups" have you joined on Facebook? | | | | Total |
|---|---|---|---|---|---|
| | 1-10 | 11-20 | 21 or more | None | |
| Males | 76 | 55 | 19 | 2 | 195 |
| | 39.0% | 36.9% | 23.1% | 1.0% | 100% |
| Females | 89 | 59 | 26 | 9 | 183 |
| | 48.6% | 32.2% | 14.2% | 4.9% | 100% |
| Total | 165 | 131 | 71 | 11 | 378 |
| | 43.7% | 34.7% | 18.8% | 2.9% | 100% |

Table 27: Chi-Square test when compare gender to the question "how much groups have you joined on Facebook?"

| | Value | Degree of freedom (df) | Assumption |
|---|---|---|---|
| Pearson Chi-Square | 11.484 | 3 | .009 |
| Likelihood Ratio | 11.902 | 3 | .008 |
| Linear-by-Linear Association | 1.543 | 1 | .214 |
| No. of valid Cases | 378 | | |

Table 28: Education level compared with "how many groups have you joined on Facebook?"

| Education Level | How many "groups" have you joined on Facebook? | | | | Total |
|---|---|---|---|---|---|
| | 1-10 | 11-20 | 21 or more | None | |
| Secondary School | 48 | 41 | 16 | 7 | 112 |
| | 42.9% | 36.6% | 14.3% | 6.3% | 100% |
| Post-Secondary | 75 | 71 | 35 | 2 | 183 |
| | 41.0% | 38.8% | 19.1% | 1.1% | 100% |
| Tertiary Level | 35 | 16 | 17 | 1 | 69 |
| | 50.7% | 23.2% | 24.6% | 1.4% | 100% |
| Vocational | 6 | 3 | 3 | 1 | 13 |
| | 46.2% | 23.1% | 23.1% | 7.7% | 100% |
| Total | 164 | 131 | 71 | 11 | 377 |
| | 43.5% | 34.7% | 18.8% | 2.9% | 100% |

Table 29: Chi-Square test when comparing education level to how many groups have they joined on Facebook.

| | Value | Degree of freedom (df) | Assumption |
|---|---|---|---|
| Pearson Chi-Square | 15.739 | 9 | .073 |
| Likelihood Ratio | 15.485 | 9 | .078 |
| Linear-by-Linear Association | .062 | 1 | .803 |
| No. of valid Cases | 377 | | |

Question 9

What application you use on Facebook?

Table 30: Age compare with how much participants use applications' such as Games.

| What is your age? | Application you use?    Games | | |
| | Yes | No | Total |
|---|---|---|---|
| 14-17 | 47 | 88 | 135 |
| | 34.8% | 65.2% | 100% |
| 18-21 | 42 | 70 | 112 |
| | 37.5% | 62.5% | 100% |
| 22-34 | 47 | 46 | 93 |
| | 50.5% | 49.5% | 100% |
| 35+ | 18 | 25 | 43 |
| | 41.9% | 58.1% | 100% |
| Total | 154 | 229 | 383 |
| | 40.2% | 59.8% | 100% |

Table 31: Chi-Square test when age is compared to participants using games application on Facebook.

| | Value | Degree of freedom (df) | Assumption |
|---|---|---|---|
| Pearson Chi-Square | 6.151 | 3 | .104 |
| Likelihood Ratio | 6.099 | 3 | .107 |
| Linear-by-Linear Association | 3.521 | 1 | .061 |
| No. of valid Cases | 383 | | |

Table 32: Age compare with participants use music Application on Facebook.

| What is your age? | Application you use?   Music | | Total |
| --- | --- | --- | --- |
| | Yes | No | |
| 14-17 | 28 | 107 | 135 |
| | 20.7% | 79.3% | 100% |
| 18-21 | 16 | 96 | 112 |
| | 14.3% | 85.7% | 100% |
| 22-34 | 17 | 76 | 93 |
| | 18.3% | 81.7% | 100% |
| 35+ | 11 | 32 | 43 |
| | 25.6% | 74.4% | 100% |
| Total | 72 | 311 | 383 |
| | 18.8% | 81.2% | 100% |

Table 33: Chi-Square test when age is compared with participants using music application on Facebook.

| | Value | Degree of freedom (df) | Assumption |
| --- | --- | --- | --- |
| Pearson Chi-Square | 3.140 | 3 | .371 |
| Likelihood Ratio | 3.137 | 3 | .371 |
| Linear-by-Linear Association | .123 | 1 | .726 |
| No. of valid Cases | 383 | | |

Table 34: Age compare with use of video application on Facebook.

| What is your age? | Application you use? Video | | |
|---|---|---|---|
| | Yes | No | Total |
| 14-17 | 41<br>30.4% | 94<br>69.6% | 135<br>100% |
| 18-21 | 23<br>20.5% | 89<br>79.5% | 112<br>100% |
| 22-34 | 22<br>18.3% | 71<br>81.7% | 93<br>100% |
| 35+ | 12<br>27.9% | 31<br>72.1% | 43<br>100% |
| Total | 98<br>25.6% | 285<br>74.4% | 383<br>100% |

Table 35: Chi-Square test for age compared to video application used on Facebook.

| | Value | Degree of freedom (df) | Assumption |
|---|---|---|---|
| Pearson Chi-Square | 3.427 | 3 | .330 |
| Likelihood Ratio | 3.441 | 3 | .328 |
| Linear-by-Linear Association | .520 | 1 | .471 |
| No. of valid Cases | 383 | | |

Table 36: Gender compared with use of game application usage.

| What is your gender? | Application you use? Games | | |
|---|---|---|---|
| | Yes | No | Total |
| Males | 58<br>29.4% | 139<br>70.6% | 197<br>100% |
| Females | 96<br>51.6% | 90<br>48.4% | 186<br>100% |
| Total | 154<br>40.2% | 229<br>59.8% | 383<br>100% |

Table 37: Chi-Square test when compare gender with Games application use on Facebook.

|  | Value | Degree of freedom (df) | Assumption |
|---|---|---|---|
| Pearson Chi-Square | 19.562 | 1 | .000 |
| Likelihood Ratio | 19.724 | 1 | .000 |
| Linear-by-Linear Association | 19.510 | 1 | .000 |
| No. of valid Cases | 383 |  |  |

Table 38: Gender compared with use of music application use on Facebook.

| What is your gender? | Application you use?   Music | | |
|---|---|---|---|
|  | Yes | No | Total |
| Males | 34 | 163 | 197 |
|  | 17.3% | 82.7% | 100% |
| Females | 38 | 148 | 186 |
|  | 20.4% | 79.6% | 100% |
| Total | 72 | 331 | 383 |
|  | 18.8% | 81.2% | 100% |

Table 39: Chi-Square test to compare gender against use of music application on Facebook.

|  | Value | Degree of freedom (df) | Assumption |
|---|---|---|---|
| Pearson Chi-Square | .630 | 1 | .427 |
| Likelihood Ratio | .630 | 1 | .427 |
| Linear-by-Linear Association | .629 | 1 | ..428 |
| No. of valid Cases | 383 |  |  |

Table 40: Gender compared with use of video application on Facebook.

| What is your gender? | Application you use?   Video | | Total |
| | Yes | No | |
|---|---|---|---|
| Males | 65 | 132 | 197 |
| | 33.0% | 67.0% | 100% |
| Females | 33 | 153 | 186 |
| | 17.7% | 82.3% | 100% |
| Total | 98 | 285 | 383 |
| | 25.6% | 74.4% | 100% |

Table 41: Chi-Square test when compare video application usage on Facebook

| | Value | Degree of freedom (df) | Assumption |
|---|---|---|---|
| Pearson Chi-Square | 11.690 | 6 | .001 |
| Likelihood Ratio | 11.876 | 6 | .001 |
| Linear-by-Linear Association | 11.660 | 1 | .001 |
| No. of valid Cases | 383 | | |

Table 42: Education level compare with use of games application on Facebook.

| Education level | Application you use?   Games | | Total |
| | Yes | No | |
|---|---|---|---|
| Secondary School | 57 | 58 | 115 |
| | 49.6% | 50.4% | 100% |
| Post-Secondary | 67 | 117 | 184 |
| | 36.4% | 63.6% | 100% |
| Tertiary Level | 24 | 46 | 70 |
| | 34.3% | 65.7% | 100% |
| Vocational | 5 | 8 | 13 |
| | 38.5% | 61.5% | 100% |
| Total | 153 | 229 | 382 |
| | 40.1% | 59.9% | 100% |

Table 43: Chi-Square Test where education level is compare to the use of games applications on Facebook.

| | Value | Degree of freedom (df) | Assumption |
|---|---|---|---|
| Pearson Chi-Square | 6.332 | 3 | .097 |
| Likelihood Ratio | 6.278 | 3 | .099 |
| Linear-by-Linear Association | 4.168 | 1 | .041 |
| No. of valid Cases | 382 | | |

Table 44: Education level compared with music application usage on Facebook.

| Education level | Application you use?    Music | | |
|---|---|---|---|
| | Yes | No | Total |
| Secondary School | 28 24.3% | 87 75.7% | 115 100% |
| Post-Secondary | 29 15.8% | 155 84.2% | 184 100% |
| Tertiary Level | 11 15.7% | 59 84.3% | 70 100% |
| Vocational | 4 30.8% | 9 69.2% | 13 100% |
| Total | 72 18.8% | 310 81.2% | 382 100% |

Table 45: Chi-Square test when comparing Education level with music application usage on Facebook.

| | Value | Degree of freedom (df) | Assumption |
|---|---|---|---|
| Pearson Chi-Square | 5.078 | 3 | .166 |
| Likelihood Ratio | 4.858 | 3 | .183 |
| Linear-by-Linear Association | .811 | 1 | .368 |
| No. of valid Cases | 382 | | |

Table 46: Video application used on Facebook compared with education level.

| Education level | Application you use? Videos | | Total |
|---|---|---|---|
| | Yes | No | |
| Secondary School | 30 | 85 | 115 |
| | 26.1% | 73.9% | 100% |
| Post-Secondary | 29 | 133 | 184 |
| | 27.7% | 72.3% | 100% |
| Tertiary Level | 12 | 58 | 70 |
| | 17.1% | 82.9% | 100% |
| Vocational | 5 | 8 | 13 |
| | 38.5% | 61.5% | 100% |
| Total | 98 | 284 | 382 |
| | 25.7% | 74.3% | 100% |

Table 47: Chi-Square test when comparing video application usage to the education level.

| | Value | Degree of freedom (df) | Assumption |
|---|---|---|---|
| Pearson Chi-Square | 4.199 | 3 | .241 |
| Likelihood Ratio | 4.338 | 3 | .227 |
| Linear-by-Linear Association | .216 | 1 | .642 |
| No. of valid Cases | 382 | | |

Question 10

Do you use Facebook on different devices?

Table 48: Participants' age is compared whether participants use a Facebook on different device.

| What is your age? | Do you use Facebook on different Devices? | | Total |
|---|---|---|---|
| | Yes | No | |
| 14-17 | 117 | 15 | 132 |
| | 88.6% | 11.4% | 100% |
| 18-21 | 103 | 9 | 112 |
| | 92.0% | 8.0% | 100% |
| 22-34 | 71 | 21 | 92 |
| | 77.2% | 22.8% | 100% |
| 35+ | 28 | 15 | 43 |
| | 65.1% | 34.9% | 100% |
| Total | 319 | 60 | 379 |
| | 84.2% | 81.2% | 100% |

Table 49: Chi-Square test where age is compare whether participants use Facebook on different device.

| | Value | Degree of freedom (df) | Assumption |
|---|---|---|---|
| Pearson Chi-Square | 22.177 | 3 | .000 |
| Likelihood Ratio | 20.573 | 3 | .000 |
| Linear-by-Linear Association | 15.811 | 1 | .000 |
| No. of valid Cases | 379 | | |

Table 50: Participants' gender is compared whether participants use a Facebook on different device.

| What is your gender? | Do you use Facebook on different Devices? | | Total |
| --- | --- | --- | --- |
| | Yes | No | |
| Males | 169 | 25 | 194 |
| | 87.1% | 12.9% | 100% |
| Females | 150 | 35 | 185 |
| | 81.1% | 18.9% | 100% |
| Total | 319 | 60 | 379 |
| | 84.2% | 15.8% | 100% |

Table 51: Chi-Square test when age is compared whether participants use Facebook on different device.

| | Value | Degree of freedom (df) | Assumption |
| --- | --- | --- | --- |
| Pearson Chi-Square | 2.586 | 1 | .108 |
| Likelihood Ratio | 2.593 | 1 | .107 |
| Linear-by-Linear Association | 2.579 | 1 | .108 |
| No. of valid Cases | 379 | | |

Table 52: Participants' education level is compared whether they use a Facebook on different device.

| Education level | Do you use Facebook on different Devices? | | Total |
| --- | --- | --- | --- |
| | Yes | No | |
| Secondary School | 94 | 20 | 114 |
| | 82.5% | 17.5% | 100% |
| Post-Secondary | 160 | 21 | 181 |
| | 88.4% | 11.6% | 100% |
| Tertiary Level | 56 | 14 | 70 |
| | 80.0% | 20.0% | 100% |
| Vocational | 8 | 5 | 13 |
| | 61.5% | 38.5% | 100% |
| Total | 318 | 60 | 378 |
| | 84.1% | 15.9% | 100% |

Table 53: Chi-Square test when comparing education level to whether they use Facebook on different device.

| | Value | Degree of freedom (df) | Assumption |
|---|---|---|---|
| Pearson Chi-Square | 8.574 | 3 | .036 |
| Likelihood Ratio | 7.600 | 3 | .055 |
| Linear-by-Linear Association | 1.494 | 1 | .222 |
| No. of valid Cases | 378 | | |

Question 11

Do you prefer communicating with friends by....?

Table 54: Type of preferred communication method is compared to the age of the participants.

| What is your age? | Do you prefer communicating with friends by... | | | | |
|---|---|---|---|---|---|
| | E-mail | Facebook | Phone | Skype | Total |
| 14-17 | 3 | 89 | 21 | 21 | 134 |
| | 2.2% | 66.4% | 15.7% | 15.7% | 100% |
| 18-21 | 2 | 80 | 23 | 6 | 111 |
| | 1.8% | 72.1 | 20.7% | 5.4% | 100% |
| 22-34 | 8 | 56 | 25 | 3 | 92 |
| | 8.7% | 60.9% | 27.2% | 3.3% | 100% |
| 35+ | 2 | 26 | 13 | 2 | 43 |
| | 4.7% | 60.5% | 30.2% | 4.7% | 100% |
| Total | 15 | 251 | 82 | 32 | 380 |
| | 3.9% | 66.1% | 21.6% | 8.4% | 100% |

Table 55: Chi-Square Test when comparing communication method to age.

| | Value | Degree of freedom (df) | Assumption |
|---|---|---|---|
| Pearson Chi-Square | 27.014 | 9 | .001 |
| Likelihood Ratio | 25.633 | 9 | .002 |
| Linear-by-Linear Association | 2.636 | 1 | .104 |
| No. of valid Cases | 380 | | |

Table 56: Type of communication method is compared to the gender of the participants.

| What is your gender? | Do you prefer communicating with friends by... | | | | Total |
|---|---|---|---|---|---|
| | Email | Facebook | Phone | Skype | |
| Males | 5 | 137 | 30 | 24 | 196 |
| | 2.6% | 69.9% | 15.3% | 12.2% | 100% |
| Females | 10 | 114 | 52 | 8 | 184 |
| | 5.4% | 62.0% | 28.3% | 4.3% | 100% |
| Total | 15 | 251 | 82 | 32 | 380 |
| | 3.9% | 66.1% | 21.6% | 8.4% | 100% |

Table 57: Chi-Square test when compare preferred communication method with gender.

| | Value | Degree of freedom (df) | Assumption |
|---|---|---|---|
| Pearson Chi-Square | 17.315 | 3 | .001 |
| Likelihood Ratio | 17.778 | 3 | .000 |
| Linear-by-Linear Association | .655 | 1 | .418 |
| No. of valid Cases | 380 | | |

Table 58: Type of communication method is compared to the education level of participants.

| Education level | Do you prefer communicating with friends by... | | | | Total |
|---|---|---|---|---|---|
| | E-mail | Facebook | Phone | Skype | |
| Secondary School | 3 | 67 | 26 | 19 | 115 |
| | 2.6% | 58.3% | 58.3% | 16.5% | 100% |
| Post-Secondary | 6 | 134 | 35 | 8 | 183 |
| | 3.3% | 73.2% | 19.1% | 4.4% | 100% |
| Tertiary Level | 6 | 40 | 18 | 4 | 68 |
| | 8.8% | 58.8% | 26.5% | 5.9% | 100% |
| Vocational | 0 | 9 | 3 | 1 | 13 |
| | .0% | 69.2% | 23.1% | 7.7% | 100% |
| Total | 15 | 250 | 82 | 32 | 379 |
| | 4.0% | 66.0% | 21.6% | 8.4% | 100% |

Table 59: Chi-Square test when education level is compared to the preferred communication method.

|  | Value | Degree of freedom (df) | Assumption |
|---|---|---|---|
| Pearson Chi-Square | 22.717 | 9 | .007 |
| Likelihood Ratio | 21.118 | 9 | .012 |
| Linear-by-Linear Association | 5.070 | 1 | .024 |
| No. of valid Cases | 379 |  |  |

Question 12

Type of friends you have on you Facebook account.

For the following statements, please state your agreement/disagreement by putting a sign on the box below 1-5, where 1 means strongly disagree, 5 means strongly agree.

Table 60: Age of participants is compare to the type of friends in this case "school friends"

| What is your age? | Type of Friends? School Friends | | | | | |
|---|---|---|---|---|---|---|
| | 1 | 2 | 3 | 4 | 5 | Total |
| 14-17 | 1 .8% | 1 .8% | 7 5.3% | 30 22.6% | 94 70.7% | 133 100% |
| 18-21 | 0 1.8% | 2 2.0% | 5 4.9% | 23 22.5% | 72 70.6% | 102 100% |
| 22-34 | 10 11.4% | 10 11.4% | 17 19.3% | 18 20.5% | 33 37.5% | 88 100% |
| 35+ | 2 45.9% | 7 20.6 | 8 23.5% | 5 14.7% | 12 35.5% | 34 100% |
| Total | 13 3.6% | 20 5.6% | 37 10.4% | 76 21.3% | 211 59.1% | 357 100% |

Table 61 : Chi-Square test when age is compared with type of friends "School friends"

| | Value | Degree of freedom (df) | Assumption |
|---|---|---|---|
| Pearson Chi-Square | 83.653 | 12 | .000 |
| Likelihood Ratio | 80.758 | 12 | .000 |
| Linear-by-Linear Association | 56.669 | 1 | .000 |
| No. of valid Cases | 357 | | |

Table 62: Age of participants is compare to the type of friends in this case "Never meet friends".

| What is your age? | Type of Friends? Friends you actually never met | | | | | |
|---|---|---|---|---|---|---|
| | 1 | 2 | 3 | 4 | 5 | Total |
| 14-17 | 44 | 23 | 12 | 11 | 9 | 99 |
| | 44.4% | 23.2% | 12.1% | 11.1% | 9.1% | 100% |
| 18-21 | 34 | 25 | 11 | 7 | 6 | 83 |
| | 41.0% | 30.1% | 13.3% | 8.4% | 7.2% | 100% |
| 22-34 | 23 | 15 | 13 | 5 | 7 | 63 |
| | 36.5% | 23.8% | 20.6% | 7.9% | 11.1% | 100% |
| 35+ | 13 | 1 | 3 | 1 | 5 | 23 |
| | 56.5% | 20.6 | 13.0% | 4.3% | 21.7% | 100% |
| Total | 114 | 64 | 39 | 24 | 27 | 268 |
| | 42.5% | 23.9% | 14.6% | 9.0% | 10.1% | 100% |

Table 63: Chi-Square test when age is compare with type of friends in this case "never meet friends".

| | Value | Degree of freedom (df) | Assumption |
|---|---|---|---|
| Pearson Chi-Square | 14.003 | 12 | .301 |
| Likelihood Ratio | 14.962 | 12 | .244 |
| Linear-by-Linear Association | .559 | 1 | .455 |
| No. of valid Cases | 268 | | |

Table 64: Age of participants is compare to the type of friends in this case "Family members".

| | Type of Friends? Family members | |
|---|---|---|

| What is your age? | 1 | 2 | 3 | 4 | 5 | Total |
|---|---|---|---|---|---|---|
| 14-17 | 26 | 27 | 21 | 19 | 27 | 120 |
| | 21.7% | 22.5% | 17.5% | 15.8% | 22.5% | 100% |
| 18-21 | 15 | 17 | 25 | 14 | 31 | 102 |
| | 14.7% | 16.7% | 24.5% | 13.7% | 30.4% | 100% |
| 22-34 | 9 | 10 | 18 | 12 | 39 | 88 |
| | 36.5% | 23.8% | 20.6% | 13.6% | 44.3% | 100% |
| 35+ | 4 | 0 | 4 | 5 | 20 | 33 |
| | 12.1% | .0% | 12.1% | 15.2% | 60.6% | 100% |
| Total | 54 | 54 | 68 | 50 | 117 | 343 |
| | 15.7% | 15.7% | 19.8% | 14.6% | 34.1% | 100% |

Table 65: Chi-Square test when age is compared with typer of friends in this case "Family members".

| | Value | Degree of freedom (df) | Assumption |
|---|---|---|---|
| Pearson Chi-Square | 31.861 | 12 | .001 |
| Likelihood Ratio | 35.986 | 12 | .000 |
| Linear-by-Linear Association | 23.026 | 1 | .000 |
| No. of valid Cases | 343 | | |

Table 66: Age of participants is compare to the type of friends in this case "old friends".

| What is your age? | Type of Friends? Old friends | | | | | |
|---|---|---|---|---|---|---|
| | 1 | 2 | 3 | 4 | 5 | Total |
| 14-17 | 6 | 24 | 42 | 30 | 23 | 125 |
| | 4.8% | 19.2% | 33.6% | 24.0% | 18.4% | 100% |
| 18-21 | 4 | 12 | 33 | 27 | 24 | 100 |
| | 4.0% | 12.0% | 33.30% | 27.0% | 24.0% | 100% |

| 22-34 | 6 | 9 | 18 | 27 | 28 | 88 |
|---|---|---|---|---|---|---|
| | 6.8% | 10.2% | 20.5% | 30.7% | 31.8% | 100% |
| 35+ | 3 | 2 | 5 | 6 | 18 | 34 |
| | 8.8% | 5.9% | 14.7% | 17.6% | 52.9% | 100% |
| Total | 19 | 47 | 98 | 90 | 93 | 347 |
| | 5.5% | 13.5% | 28.2% | 25.9% | 26.8% | 100% |

Table 67: Chi-Square test when comparing age to types of friends in this case "Old friends".

| | Value | Degree of freedom (df) | Assumption |
|---|---|---|---|
| Pearson Chi-Square | 27.940 | 12 | .006 |
| Likelihood Ratio | 27.062 | 12 | .008 |
| Linear-by-Linear Association | 11.078 | 1 | .001 |
| No. of valid Cases | 347 | | |

Table 68: Age of participants is compare to the type of friends in this case "foreign friends".

| What is your age? | Type of Friends? Foreign Friends | | | | | |
|---|---|---|---|---|---|---|
| | 1 | 2 | 3 | 4 | 5 | Total |
| 14-17 | 43 | 27 | 18 | 5 | 7 | 100 |
| | 43.0% | 27.0% | 18.0% | 5.0% | 7.0% | 100% |
| 18-21 | 26 | 26 | 16 | 9 | 11 | 88 |
| | 29.5% | 29.5% | 18.2% | 10.2% | 12.5% | 100% |
| 22-34 | 26 | 18 | 16 | 10 | 8 | 78 |
| | 33.3% | 23.1% | 20.5% | 12.8% | 10.3% | 100% |
| 35+ | 8 | 5 | 5 | 3 | 9 | 30 |
| | 26.7% | 16.7% | 16.7% | 10.0% | 30.0% | 100% |
| Total | 103 | 76 | 55 | 27 | 35 | 296 |
| | 34.8% | 25.7% | 18.6% | 9.1% | 11.8% | 100% |

|  | Value | Degree of freedom (df) | Assumption |
|---|---|---|---|
| Pearson Chi-Square | 18.947 | 12 | .090 |
| Likelihood Ratio | 17.066 | 12 | .147 |
| Linear-by-Linear Association | 10.149 | 1 | .001 |
| No. of valid Cases | 296 | | |

Table 69: Chi-Square test when compare type of friends in this case "Foreign friends".

Table 70: Gender of participants is compared to the type of friends in this case "School friends".

| What is your Gender? | Type of Friend? School Friends | | | | | |
|---|---|---|---|---|---|---|
| | 1 | 2 | 3 | 4 | 5 | Total |
| Males | 7 | 11 | 18 | 42 | 110 | 188 |
| | 3.7% | 5.9% | 9.6% | 22.3% | 58.5% | 100% |
| Females | 6 | 9 | 1 | 34 | 101 | 169 |
| | 3.6% | 5.3% | 11.2% | 20.1% | 59.8% | 100% |
| Total | 13 | 20 | 37 | 76 | 211 | 357 |
| | 3.6% | 5.6% | 10.4% | 21.3% | 59.1% | 100% |

Table 71: Chi-Square test when gender is compare to the type of friends in this case "School Friends".

|  | Value | Degree of freedom (df) | Assumption |
|---|---|---|---|
| Pearson Chi-Square | .520 | 4 | .972 |
| Likelihood Ratio | .520 | 4 | .971 |
| Linear-by-Linear Association | .010 | 1 | .920 |
| No. of valid Cases | 357 | | |

Table 72: Gender of participants is compare to the type of friends in this case "Never meet friends".

| What is your Gender? | Type of Friend? you actually never met | | | | | Total |
|---|---|---|---|---|---|---|
| | 1 | 2 | 3 | 4 | 5 | |
| Males | 57 | 41 | 22 | 15 | 20 | 155 |
| | 36.8% | 26.5% | 14.2% | 9.7% | 12.9% | 100% |
| Females | 57 | 23 | 17 | 9 | 7 | 113 |
| | 50.4% | 20.4% | 15.0% | 8.0% | 6.2% | 100% |
| Total | 114 | 64 | 39 | 24 | 27 | 268 |
| | 42.5% | 23.9% | 14.6% | 9.0% | 10.1% | 100% |

Table 73: Chi-Square test when compare gender with type of friends in this case " never meet friends".

| | Value | Degree of freedom (df) | Assumption |
|---|---|---|---|
| Pearson Chi-Square | 7.054 | 4 | .133 |
| Likelihood Ratio | 7.208 | 4 | .125 |
| Linear-by-Linear Association | 4.797 | 1 | .029 |
| No. of valid Cases | 268 | | |

Table 74: Gender of participants is compared to the type of friends in this case "Family members"

| What is your Gender? | Type of Friend? Family Members | | | | | Total |
|---|---|---|---|---|---|---|
| | 1 | 2 | 3 | 4 | 5 | |
| Males | 33 | 30 | 43 | 30 | 41 | 177 |
| | 18.6% | 16.9% | 24.3% | 16.9% | 23.3% | 100% |
| Females | 21 | 24 | 25 | 20 | 76 | 166 |
| | 12.7% | 14.5% | 15.1% | 12.0% | 45.8% | 100% |
| Total | 54 | 54 | 68 | 50 | 117 | 343 |
| | 15.7% | 15.7% | 19.8% | 14.6% | 34.1% | 100% |

Table 75: Chi-Square test when gender is compared with type of friends in this case "family members".

|  | Value | Degree of freedom (df) | Assumption |
|---|---|---|---|
| Pearson Chi-Square | 20.236 | 4 | .000 |
| Likelihood Ratio | 20.472 | 4 | .000 |
| Linear-by-Linear Association | 11.822 | 1 | .001 |
| No. of valid Cases | 343 |  |  |

Table 76: Gender of participants is compared to the type of friends in this case "old friends".

| What is your Gender? | Type of Friend? Old Friends | | | | | |
|---|---|---|---|---|---|---|
|  | 1 | 2 | 3 | 4 | 5 | Total |
| Males | 10 | 32 | 52 | 55 | 32 | 181 |
|  | 5.5% | 17.7% | 28.7% | 30.4% | 17.7% | 100% |
| Females | 9 | 15 | 46 | 35 | 61 | 166 |
|  | 5.4% | 9.0% | 27.7% | 21.1% | 36.7% | 100% |
| Total | 19 | 47 | 98 | 90 | 93 | 357 |
|  | 5.5% | 13.5% | 28.2% | 25.9% | 26.8% | 100% |

Table 77: Chi-Square test gender is compared with type of friends in this case "old friends".

|  | Value | Degree of freedom (df) | Assumption |
|---|---|---|---|
| Pearson Chi-Square | 19.444 | 4 | .001 |
| Likelihood Ratio | 19.740 | 4 | .001 |
| Linear-by-Linear Association | 8.865 | 1 | .003 |
| No. of valid Cases | 347 |  |  |

Table 78: Gender of participants is compared to the type of friends in this case "foreign friends".

| What is your Gender? | Type of Friend? Foreign Friends | | | | | Total |
|---|---|---|---|---|---|---|
| | 1 | 2 | 3 | 4 | 5 | |
| Males | 61 | 43 | 27 | 15 | 11 | 157 |
| | 38.9% | 27.4% | 17.2% | 9.6% | 7.0% | 100% |
| Females | 42 | 33 | 28 | 12 | 24 | 139 |
| | 30.2% | 23.7% | 20.1% | 8.6% | 17.3% | 100% |
| Total | 103 | 76 | 55 | 27 | 35 | 296 |
| | 34.8% | 25.7% | 18.6% | 9.1% | 11.8% | 100% |

Table 79: Chi-Square test is compared to type of friends in this case "foreign friends".

| | Value | Degree of freedom (df) | Assumption |
|---|---|---|---|
| Pearson Chi-Square | 8.939 | 4 | .063 |
| Likelihood Ratio | 9.048 | 4 | .060 |
| Linear-by-Linear Association | 6.621 | 1 | .010 |
| No. of valid Cases | 296 | | |

Table 80: Education level of participants is compared to the type of friends in this case "School friends".

| Education level | Type of Friend? School Friends | | | | | Total |
|---|---|---|---|---|---|---|
| | 1 | 2 | 3 | 4 | 5 | |
| Secondary School | 5 | 9 | 11 | 21 | 60 | 106 |
| | 4.7% | 8.5% | 10.4% | 19.8% | 56.6% | 100% |
| Post-Secondary | 4 | 2 | 13 | 36 | 118 | 173 |
| | 2.3% | 1.2% | 7.5% | 20.8% | 68.2% | 100% |
| Tertiary Level | 3 | 6 | 12 | 14 | 29 | 64 |
| | 4.7% | 9.4% | 18.8% | 21.9% | 45.3% | 100% |
| Vocational | 1 | 3 | 1 | 4 | 4 | 13 |
| | 7.7% | 23.1% | 7.7% | 30.8% | 30.8% | 100% |
| Total | 13 | 20 | 37 | 75 | 211 | 356 |

| | 3.7% | 5.6% | 10.4% | 21.1% | 59.3% | 100% |
|---|---|---|---|---|---|---|

Table 81: Chi-Square test when education level is compare to type of friends in this case "school friends".

| | Value | Degree of freedom (df) | Assumption |
|---|---|---|---|
| Pearson Chi-Square | 31.099 | 12 | .002 |
| Likelihood Ratio | 30.139 | 12 | .002 |
| Linear-by-Linear Association | 2.940 | 1 | .086 |
| No. of valid Cases | 356 | | |

Table 82: Education level of participants is compare to the type of friends in this case "never meet friends".

| Education level | Type of Friend? Friends you never met | | | | | |
|---|---|---|---|---|---|---|
| | 1 | 2 | 3 | 4 | 5 | Total |
| Secondary School | 27 | 17 | 16 | 10 | 8 | 78 |
| | 34.6% | 21.8% | 20.5% | 12.8% | 10.3% | 100% |
| Post-Secondary | 63 | 34 | 13 | 10 | 14 | 134 |
| | 47.0% | 25.4% | 9.7% | 7.5% | 10.4% | 100% |
| Tertiary Level | 19 | 10 | 7 | 3 | 4 | 43 |
| | 44.2% | 23.3% | 16.3% | 7.0% | 9.3% | 100% |
| Vocational | 4 | 3 | 3 | 1 | 1 | 12 |
| | 33.3% | 25.0% | 25.0% | 8.3% | 8.3% | 100% |
| Total | 113 | 64 | 39 | 24 | 27 | 267 |
| | 42.3% | 24.0% | 14.6% | 9.0% | 10.1% | 100% |

Table 83: Chi-Square test when comparing education level to type of friends in this case "School friends".

| | Value | Degree of freedom (df) | Assumption |
|---|---|---|---|
| Pearson Chi-Square | 9.277 | 12 | .679 |
| Likelihood Ratio | 9.166 | 12 | .689 |

| | | | |
|---|---|---|---|
| Linear-by-Linear Association | .921 | 1 | .337 |
| No. of valid Cases | 267 | | |

Table 84: Education level of participants is compared to the type of friends in this case "Family members"

| Education level | Type of Friend? Family members | | | | | |
|---|---|---|---|---|---|---|
| | 1 | 2 | 3 | 4 | 5 | Total |
| Secondary School | 17 | 16 | 14 | 14 | 40 | 101 |
| | 16.8% | 21.8% | 15.8% | 13.9% | 39.6% | 100% |
| Post-Secondary | 30 | 29 | 33 | 27 | 46 | 165 |
| | 18.2% | 17.6% | 20.0% | 16.4% | 27.9% | 100% |
| Tertiary Level | 6 | 8 | 18 | 5 | 26 | 63 |
| | 9.5% | 12.7% | 28.6% | 7.9% | 41.3% | 100% |
| Vocational | 1 | 1 | 2 | 4 | 5 | 13 |
| | 7.7% | 7.7% | 15.4% | 30.8% | 38.5% | 100% |
| Total | 54 | 54 | 67 | 50 | 117 | 342 |
| | 15.8% | 15.8% | 19.6% | 14.6% | 34.2% | 100% |

Table 85: Chi-Square test when comparing type of friends in this case "Family members" to Education level.

| | Value | Degree of freedom (df) | Assumption |
|---|---|---|---|
| Pearson Chi-Square | 16.851 | 12 | .155 |
| Likelihood Ratio | 17.073 | 12 | .147 |
| Linear-by-Linear Association | .790 | 1 | .374 |
| No. of valid Cases | 342 | | |

Table 86: Education level of participants is compare to the type of friends in this case "old friends".

| Education level | Type of Friend? Old friends | | | | | |
|---|---|---|---|---|---|---|
| | 1 | 2 | 3 | 4 | 5 | Total |
| Secondary School | 7 | 18 | 23 | 21 | 30 | 99 |

| | 7.1% | 18.2% | 23.2% | 21.2% | 30.3% | 100% |
|---|---|---|---|---|---|---|
| Post-Secondary | 6 | 23 | 58 | 46 | 37 | 170 |
| | 3.5% | 13.5% | 34.1% | 27.1% | 21.8% | 100% |
| Tertiary Level | 6 | 6 | 16 | 15 | 21 | 64 |
| | 9.4% | 9.4% | 25.0% | 23.4% | 32.8% | 100% |
| Vocational | 0 | 0 | 1 | 7 | 5 | 13 |
| | .0% | .0% | 7.7% | 53.8% | 38.5% | 100% |
| Total | 19 | 47 | 98 | 89 | 93 | 346 |
| | 5.5% | 13.6% | 28.3% | 25.7% | 26.9% | 100% |

Table 87: Chi-Square test when comparing type of friends in this case "Old friends" to the education level.

| | Value | Degree of freedom (df) | Assumption |
|---|---|---|---|
| Pearson Chi-Square | 21.980 | 12 | .038 |
| Likelihood Ratio | 24.040 | 12 | .020 |
| Linear-by-Linear Association | 2.805 | 1 | .094 |
| No. of valid Cases | 346 | | |

Table 88: Education level of participants is compared to the type of friends in this case "foreign friends".

| Education level | Type of Friend? Foreign friends | | | | | |
|---|---|---|---|---|---|---|
| | 1 | 2 | 3 | 4 | 5 | Total |
| Secondary School | 30 | 15 | 20 | 6 | 8 | 79 |
| | 38.0% | 19.0% | 25.3% | 7.6% | 10.1% | 100% |

| Post-Secondary | 52 | 40 | 20 | 14 | 18 | 144 |
|---|---|---|---|---|---|---|
| | 47.0% | 25.4% | 9.7% | 7.5% | 10.4% | 100% |
| Tertiary Level | 18 | 18 | 11 | 6 | 6 | 59 |
| | 30.5% | 30.5% | 18.6% | 10.2% | 10.2% | 100% |
| Vocational | 2 | 3 | 4 | 1 | 3 | 13 |
| | 15.4% | 23.1% | 30.8% | 7.7% | 23.1% | 100% |
| Total | 102 | 76 | 55 | 27 | 35 | 295 |
| | 34.6% | 25.8% | 18.6% | 9.2% | 11.9% | 100% |

Table 89: Chi-Square test to compare education level to type of friends in this case "foreign friends".

| | Value | Degree of freedom (df) | Assumption |
|---|---|---|---|
| Pearson Chi-Square | 11.002 | 12 | .529 |
| Likelihood Ratio | 11.016 | 12 | .528 |
| Linear-by-Linear Association | 1.237 | 1 | .266 |
| No. of valid Cases | 295 | | |

Question 13

Who can see your profile?

Table 90: "Who can see your profile?" question is compared to age.

| What is your age? | Who can see you Profile? | | | |
|---|---|---|---|---|
| | Everyone | Friends of Friends | Only friends | |
| 14-17 | 15 11.3% | 37 27.8% | 81 60.9% | 133 100% |
| 18-21 | 12 10.9% | 15 13.6% | 83 75.5% | 110 100% |
| 22-34 | 9 9.8% | 14 15.2% | 69 75.0% | 92 100% |
| 35+ | 11 26.2% | 5 11.9% | 26 61.9% | 42 100% |
| Total | 47 12.5% | 71 18.8% | 259 68.7% | 377 100% |

Table 91: Chi-Square test when comparing age to "Who can see your profile?".

| | Value | Degree of freedom (df) | Assumption |
|---|---|---|---|
| Pearson Chi-Square | 18.953 | 6 | .004 |
| Likelihood Ratio | 17.126 | 6 | .009 |
| Linear-by-Linear Association | .00 | 1 | .990 |
| No. of valid Cases | 377 | | |

Table 92: "Who can see you profile?" question is compared to gender.

| What is your gender? | Who can see your profile? | | | |
|---|---|---|---|---|
| | Everyone | Friends of friends | Only friends | Total |
| Males | 32 16.4% | 52 26.7% | 111 56.9% | 195 100% |
| Females | 15 8.2% | 19 10.4% | 148 81.3% | 182 100% |
| Total | 47 12.5% | 71 18.8% | 259 68.7% | 377 100% |

Table 93: Chi-Square test when comparing gender to question "Who can see your profile?"

| | Value | Degree of freedom (df) | Assumption |
|---|---|---|---|
| Pearson Chi-Square | 26.356 | 2 | .000 |
| Likelihood Ratio | 27.090 | 2 | .000 |
| Linear-by-Linear Association | 20.095 | 1 | .000 |
| No. of valid Cases | 377 | | |

Table 94: "Who can see you profile?" question is compared to education level.

| Education level | Who can see you Profile? | | | |
|---|---|---|---|---|
| | Everyone | Friends of friends | Only friends | Total |
| Secondary School | 21 | 23 | 68 | 112 |
| | 18.8% | 20.5% | 60.7% | 100% |
| Post-Secondary | 17 | 38 | 127 | 182 |
| | 9.3% | 20.9% | 69.8% | 100% |
| Tertiary Level | 4 | 9 | 56 | 69 |
| | 5.8% | 13.0% | 81.2% | 100% |
| Vocational | 5 | 1 | 7 | 13 |
| | 38.5% | 7.7% | 53.8% | 100% |
| Total | 47 | 71 | 258 | 376 |
| | 12.5% | 18.9% | 68.6% | 100% |

Table 95: Chi-Square test when comparing education level to question "Who can see your profile?"

| | Value | Degree of freedom (df) | Assumption |
|---|---|---|---|
| Pearson Chi-Square | 20.148 | 6 | .003 |
| Likelihood Ratio | 18.294 | 6 | .006 |
| Linear-by-Linear Association | 2.975 | 1 | .085 |
| No. of valid Cases | 376 | | |

Question 14

What do you typically use Facebook for?
For the following statements, please state your agreement/disagreement by putting a sign on
the box below 1-5, where 1 means strongly disagree, 5 means strongly agree.

Table 96: Facebook preferences age is compare "To communicate with friends".

| What is your age? | To Communicate with friends | | | | | |
|---|---|---|---|---|---|---|
| | 1 | 2 | 3 | 4 | 5 | Total |
| 14-17 | 1 | 1 | 9 | 18 | 101 | 130 |
| | .8% | .8% | 6.9% | 13.8% | 77.7% | 100% |
| 18-21 | 0 | 2 | 5 | 15 | 81 | 103 |
| | .0% | 1.9% | 4.9% | 14.6% | 78.6% | 100% |
| 22-34 | 3 | 1 | 14 | 20 | 49 | 87 |
| | 3.4% | 1.1% | 16.1% | 23.0% | 56.3% | 100% |
| 35+ | 3 | 1 | 9 | 4 | 17 | 34 |
| | 8.8% | 2.9% | 26.5% | 11.8% | 50.0% | 100% |
| Total | 7 | 5 | 37 | 57 | 248 | 354 |
| | 2.0% | 1.4% | 10.5% | 16.1% | 70.1% | 100% |

Table 97: Chi-Square test where age is compare to communicate with friend's preference.

| | Value | Degree of freedom (df) | Assumption |
|---|---|---|---|
| Pearson Chi-Square | 38.811 | 12 | .000 |
| Likelihood Ratio | 35.316 | 12 | .000 |
| Linear-by-Linear Association | 34.271 | 1 | .000 |
| No. of valid Cases | 354 | | |

Table 98: Facebook preferences compared "To communicate with Family members".

| What is your age? | To Communicate with family members | | | | | |
|---|---|---|---|---|---|---|
| | 1 | 2 | 3 | 4 | 5 | Total |
| 14-17 | 41 | 28 | 15 | 5 | 10 | 99 |
| | 41.4% | 28.3% | 15.2% | 5.1% | 10.1% | 100% |
| 18-21 | 24 | 20 | 19 | 12 | 10 | 85 |
| | 28.2% | 23.5% | 22.4% | 14.1% | 11.8% | 100% |
| 22-34 | 19 | 10 | 15 | 9 | 27 | 80 |
| | 23.8% | 12.5% | 18.8% | 11.3% | 33.8% | 100% |
| 35+ | 8 | 3 | 0 | 1 | 15 | 27 |
| | 29.6% | 11.1% | .0% | 3.7% | 55.6% | 100% |
| Total | 92 | 61 | 49 | 27 | 62 | 291 |
| | 31.6% | 21.0% | 16.8% | 9.3% | 21.3% | 100% |

Table 99: Chi-Square test where age is compared with "To communicate with Family members" preference.

| | Value | Degree of freedom (df) | Assumption |
|---|---|---|---|
| Pearson Chi-Square | 53.554 | 12 | .000 |
| Likelihood Ratio | 55.286 | 12 | .000 |
| Linear-by-Linear Association | 27.870 | 1 | .000 |
| No. of valid Cases | 291 | | |

Table 100: Facebook where age is compare "To communicate with friends out of the country" preference.

| What is your age? | To Communicate friends out of the country | | | | | Total |
|---|---|---|---|---|---|---|
| | 1 | 2 | 3 | 4 | 5 | |
| 14-17 | 36 | 18 | 14 | 4 | 8 | 99 |
| | 45.0% | 22.5% | 17.5% | 5.0% | 10.0% | 100% |
| 18-21 | 29 | 15 | 17 | 9 | 12 | 82 |
| | 35.4% | 18.3% | 20.7% | 11.0% | 14.6% | 100% |
| 22-34 | 20 | 11 | 19 | 10 | 10 | 70 |
| | 28.6% | 15.7% | 27.1% | 14.3% | 14.3% | 100% |
| 35+ | 6 | 2 | 3 | 6 | 9 | 26 |
| | 23.1% | 7.7% | 11.5% | 23.1% | 34.6% | 100% |
| Total | 91 | 46 | 53 | 29 | 39 | 258 |
| | 35.5% | 17.8% | 20.5% | 11.2% | 15.1% | 100% |

Table 101: Chi-Square test done where age is compare "To communicate with friends out of the country" preference.

| | Value | Degree of freedom (df) | Assumption |
|---|---|---|---|
| Pearson Chi-Square | 24.234 | 12 | .019 |
| Likelihood Ratio | 13.042 | 12 | .027 |
| Linear-by-Linear Association | 15.198 | 1 | .000 |
| No. of valid Cases | 258 | | |

Table 102: Facebook preference "To play games" compared against age.

| What is your age? | To play games | | | | | |
|---|---|---|---|---|---|---|
| | 1 | 2 | 3 | 4 | 5 | Total |
| 14-17 | 33 | 13 | 9 | 5 | 4 | 64 |
| | 51.6% | 20.3% | 14.1% | 7.8% | 6.3% | 100% |
| 18-21 | 30 | 8 | 8 | 5 | 7 | 58 |
| | 51.7% | 13.8% | 13.8% | 8.6% | 12.1% | 100% |
| 22-34 | 21 | 7 | 9 | 5 | 15 | 57 |
| | 36.8% | 12.3% | 15.8% | 8.8% | 26.3% | 100% |
| 35+ | 7 | 0 | 2 | 0 | 10 | 19 |
| | 36.8% | .0% | 10.5% | .0% | 52.6% | 100% |
| Total | 91 | 28 | 28 | 15 | 36 | 198 |
| | 46.0% | 14.1% | 14.1% | 7.6% | 18.2% | 100% |

Table 103: Chi-Square test done to compare preference "To play games" against age.

| | | Value | Degree of freedom (df) | Assumption |
|---|---|---|---|---|
| Pearson Chi-Square | | 29.391 | 12 | .003 |
| Likelihood Ratio | | 30.780 | 12 | .002 |
| Linear-by-Linear Association | | 14.975 | 1 | .000 |
| No. of valid Cases | | 198 | | |

Table 104: Facebook preference "To share photos or videos" compared against age.

| What is your age? | To share photos or videos | | | | | |
|---|---|---|---|---|---|---|
| | 1 | 2 | 3 | 4 | 5 | Total |
| 14-17 | 21 | 17 | 23 | 30 | 18 | 109 |
| | 19.3% | 15.6% | 21.1% | 27.5% | 16.5% | 100% |
| 18-21 | 14 | 14 | 26 | 16 | 10 | 80 |
| | 17.5% | 17.5% | 32.5% | 20.0% | 12.5% | 100% |
| 22-34 | 14 | 12 | 19 | 12 | 14 | 71 |
| | 19.7% | 16.9% | 26.8% | 16.9% | 19.7% | 100% |
| 35+ | 7 | 3 | 4 | 4 | 8 | 26 |
| | 26.9% | 11.5% | 15.4% | 15.4% | 30.8% | 100% |
| Total | 56 | 46 | 72 | 62 | 50 | 286 |
| | 19.6% | 16.1% | 25.2% | 21.7% | 17.5% | 100% |

Table 105: Chi-Square test done to compare preference "to share photos or videos" against age.

| | Value | Degree of freedom (df) | Assumption |
|---|---|---|---|
| Pearson Chi-Square | 11.930 | 12 | .451 |
| Likelihood Ratio | 11.564 | 12 | .481 |
| Linear-by-Linear Association | .003 | 1 | .959 |
| No. of valid Cases | 286 | | |

Table 106: Compare preference "To communicate with friends" against age.

| What is your gender? | To communicate with friends? | | | | | |
|---|---|---|---|---|---|---|
| | 1 | 2 | 3 | 4 | 5 | Total |
| Males | 2 | 2 | 18 | 35 | 132 | 189 |
| | 16.4% | 1.1% | 9.5% | 18.5% | 69.8% | 100% |
| Females | 5 | 3 | 19 | 22 | 116 | 165 |
| | 3.0% | 1.8% | 11.5% | 13.3% | 70.3% | 100% |
| Total | 7 | 5 | 37 | 57 | 248 | 354 |
| | 2.0% | 1.4% | 10.5% | 16.1% | 70.1% | 100% |

Table 107: Chi-Square test where age is compared against "To communicate with friends" preference.

| | Value | Degree of freedom (df) | Assumption |
|---|---|---|---|
| Pearson Chi-Square | 3.901 | 4 | .420 |
| Likelihood Ratio | 3.952 | 4 | .412 |
| Linear-by-Linear Association | .904 | 1 | .342 |
| No. of valid Cases | 354 | | |

Table 108: Preference "To communicate with family members" is compared to gender.

| What is your gender? | To communicate with family members? | | | | | |
|---|---|---|---|---|---|---|
| | 1 | 2 | 3 | 4 | 5 | Total |
| Males | 52 | 38 | 23 | 13 | 22 | 148 |
| | 35.1% | 25.7% | 15.5% | 8.8% | 14.9% | 100% |
| Females | 40 | 23 | 19 | 14 | 40 | 143 |
| | 28.8% | 16.1% | 18.2% | 9.8% | 28.0% | 100% |
| Total | 92 | 61 | 49 | 27 | 62 | 291 |
| | 31.6% | 21.0% | 16.8% | 9.3% | 21.3% | 100% |

Table 109: Chi-Square test to compare age with "To communicate with family member" preference.

| | Value | Degree of freedom (df) | Assumption |
|---|---|---|---|
| Pearson Chi-Square | 10.617 | 4 | .031 |
| Likelihood Ratio | 10.733 | 4 | .030 |
| Linear-by-Linear Association | 8.188 | 1 | .004 |
| No. of valid Cases | 291 | | |

Table 110: "To communicate with old friends" preference compared against gender.

| What is your gender? | To communicate with old friends? | | | | | |
|---|---|---|---|---|---|---|
| | 1 | 2 | 3 | 4 | 5 | Total |
| Males | 41 | 38 | 42 | 22 | 18 | 161 |
| | 25.5% | 23.6% | 26.1% | 13.7% | 11.2% | 100% |
| Females | 5 | 3 | 19 | 22 | 116 | 152 |
| | 21.7% | 17.8% | 22.4% | 11.2% | 27.0% | 100% |
| Total | 74 | 65 | 76 | 39 | 59 | 313 |
| | 23.6% | 20.8% | 24.3% | 12.5% | 18.8% | 100% |

Table 111: Chi-Square test done to compare gender against "to communicate with old friends preference.

| | Value | Degree of freedom (df) | Assumption |
|---|---|---|---|
| Pearson Chi-Square | 12.928 | 4 | .012 |
| Likelihood Ratio | 13.173 | 4 | .010 |
| Linear-by-Linear Association | 7.024 | 1 | .008 |
| No. of valid Cases | 313 | | |

Table 112 "To communicate with friends out of the country" preference is compared to gender.

| What is your gender? | To communicate with friends out of the country | | | | | |
|---|---|---|---|---|---|---|
| | 1 | 2 | 3 | 4 | 5 | Total |
| Males | 55 | 23 | 24 | 17 | 11 | 130 |
| | 42.3% | 17.7% | 18.5% | 13.1% | 8.5% | 100% |
| Females | 36 | 23 | 29 | 12 | 28 | 128 |
| | 28.1% | 18.0% | 22.7% | 9.4% | 21.9% | 100% |
| Total | 91 | 46 | 53 | 29 | 39 | 258 |
| | 35.3% | 17.8% | 20.5% | 11.2% | 15.1% | 100% |

Table 113: Chi-Square test is done to compare "To communicate with friends out of the country" preference against gender.

|  | Value | Degree of freedom (df) | Assumption |
|---|---|---|---|
| Pearson Chi-Square | 12.696 | 4 | .013 |
| Likelihood Ratio | 12.984 | 4 | .01 |
| Linear-by-Linear Association | 8.077 | 1 | .004 |
| No. of valid Cases | 258 |  |  |

Table 114: "To play games" preference compared to Gender.

| What is your gender? | To play games | | | | | |
|---|---|---|---|---|---|---|
|  | 1 | 2 | 3 | 4 | 5 | Total |
| Males | 51 | 19 | 13 | 7 | 11 | 101 |
|  | 50.5% | 18.8% | 12.9% | 6.9% | 10.9% | 100% |
| Females | 40 | 9 | 15 | 8 | 25 | 97 |
|  | 41.2% | 9.3% | 15.5% | 8.2% | 25.8% | 100% |
| Total | 91 | 28 | 28 | 15 | 36 | 198 |
|  | 46.0% | 14.1% | 14.1% | 7.6% | 18.2% | 100% |

Table 115: Chi-Square test done to compare gender against "To play games2 preference.

|  | Value | Degree of freedom (df) | Assumption |
|---|---|---|---|
| Pearson Chi-Square | 10.479 | 4 | .033 |
| Likelihood Ratio | 10.704 | 4 | .030 |
| Linear-by-Linear Association | 7.181 | 1 | .007 |
| No. of valid Cases | 198 |  |  |

Table 116: Gender is compare "To share photos or videos" preference.

| What is your gender? | Share photos or videos? | | | | | |
|---|---|---|---|---|---|---|
| | 1 | 2 | 3 | 4 | 5 | Total |
| Males | 32 | 25 | 44 | 37 | 20 | 158 |
| | 20.3% | 15.8% | 27.8% | 23.4% | 12.7% | 100% |
| Females | 24 | 21 | 28 | 25 | 30 | 128 |
| | 18.8% | 16.4% | 21.9% | 19.5% | 23.4% | 100% |
| Total | 56 | 46 | 72 | 62 | 50 | 286 |
| | 19.6% | 16.1% | 25.2% | 21.7% | 17.5% | 100% |

Table 117: Chi-Square test done to compare preference "To share photos or videos" against gender.

| | Value | Degree of freedom (df) | Assumption |
|---|---|---|---|
| Pearson Chi-Square | 6.294 | 4 | .178 |
| Likelihood Ratio | 6.279 | 4 | .179 |
| Linear-by-Linear Association | 1.530 | 1 | .216 |
| No. of valid Cases | 286 | | |

Table 118: Education level is compare "To communicate with friends" preference.

| Education level | To communicate with friends | | | | | |
|---|---|---|---|---|---|---|
| | 1 | 2 | 3 | 4 | 5 | Total |
| Secondary School | 3 | 3 | 7 | 14 | 75 | 102 |
| | 2.9% | 2.9% | 6.9% | 13.7% | 73.5% | 100% |
| Post-Secondary | 3 | 0 | 13 | 26 | 131 | 173 |
| | 1.7% | .0% | 7.5% | 15.0% | 75.7% | 100% |
| Tertiary Level | 1 | 1 | 14 | 13 | 36 | 65 |
| | 1.5% | 7.7% | 21.5% | 20.0% | 55.4% | 100% |
| Vocational | 0 | 1 | 2 | 4 | 6 | 13 |
| | .0% | 7.7% | 15.4% | 30.8% | 46.2% | 100% |
| Total | 7 | 5 | 36 | 57 | 248 | 353 |
| | 2.0% | 1.4% | 10.2% | 16.1% | 70.3% | 100% |

Table 119: Chi-Square test done to compare "To communicate with Friends" preference to education level.

| | Value | Degree of freedom (df) | Assumption |
|---|---|---|---|
| Pearson Chi-Square | 26.305 | 12 | .010 |
| Likelihood Ratio | 24.821 | 12 | .016 |
| Linear-by-Linear Association | 4.079 | 1 | .043 |
| No. of valid Cases | 353 | | |

Table 120: "To communicate with family members" preference is compared against education level.

| Education level | To communicate with family members | | | | | |
|---|---|---|---|---|---|---|
| | 1 | 2 | 3 | 4 | 5 | Total |
| Secondary School | 26 | 19 | 10 | 9 | 18 | 82 |
| | 31.7% | 23.2% | 12.2% | 11.0% | 22.0% | 100% |
| Post-Secondary | 51 | 31 | 26 | 9 | 24 | 141 |
| | 36.2% | 22.0% | 18.4% | 6.4% | 17.0% | 100% |
| Tertiary Level | 12 | 11 | 10 | 6 | 17 | 56 |
| | 21.4% | 19.6% | 17.9% | 10.7% | 30.4% | 100% |
| Vocational | 3 | 0 | 2 | 3 | 3 | 11 |
| | 27.3% | .0% | 18.2% | 27.3% | 27.3% | 100% |
| Total | 92 | 61 | 48 | 27 | 62 | 290 |
| | 31.7% | 21.0% | 16.6% | 9.3% | 21.4% | 100% |

Table 121: Chi-Square test done to compare "To communicate with family members" preference against education level.

| | Value | Degree of freedom (df) | Assumption |
|---|---|---|---|
| Pearson Chi-Square | 15.769 | 12 | .202 |
| Likelihood Ratio | 17.032 | 12 | .148 |
| Linear-by-Linear Association | 3.006 | 1 | .083 |
| No. of valid Cases | 290 | | |

Table 122: Education level is compared against "To communicate with old friends" preference.

| Education level | To communicate with old friends | | | | | |
|---|---|---|---|---|---|---|
| | 1 | 2 | 3 | 4 | 5 | Total |
| Secondary School | 21 | 21 | 22 | 12 | 15 | 91 |
| | 23.1% | 23.1% | 24.2% | 13.2% | 16.5% | 100% |
| Post-Secondary | 36 | 31 | 35 | 20 | 26 | 148 |
| | 24.3% | 20.9% | 23.6% | 13.5% | 17.6% | 100% |
| Tertiary Level | 14 | 13 | 15 | 4 | 15 | 61 |
| | 23.0% | 21.3% | 24.6% | 6.6% | 24.6% | 100% |
| Vocational | 3 | 0 | 4 | 2 | 3 | 12 |
| | 25.0% | .0% | 33.3% | 16.7% | 25.0% | 100% |
| Total | 74 | 65 | 76 | 38 | 59 | 312 |
| | 23.7% | 20.8% | 24.4% | 12.2% | 18.9% | 100% |

Table 123: Chi-Square test done to compare education level against "To communicate with old Friends" preference.

| | Value | Degree of freedom (df) | Assumption |
|---|---|---|---|
| Pearson Chi-Square | 6.994 | 12 | .858 |
| Likelihood Ratio | 9.641 | 12 | .647 |
| Linear-by-Linear Association | .712 | 1 | .399 |
| No. of valid Cases | 312 | | |

71

Table 124: Education level is compared against "To share photos or videos" preference.

| Education level | To share photos or videos | | | | | |
|---|---|---|---|---|---|---|
| | 1 | 2 | 3 | 4 | 5 | Total |
| Secondary School | 12 14.0% | 16 18.6% | 22 25.6% | 20 23.3% | 16 18.6% | 86 100% |
| Post-Secondary | 26 19.1% | 20 14.7% | 37 27.26% | 31 22.8% | 22 16.2% | 136 100% |
| Tertiary Level | 15 29.4% | 10 19.6% | 8 15.7% | 10 19.6% | 8 15.7% | 51 100% |
| Vocational | 2 16.7% | 0 .0% | 5 41.7% | 1 8.3% | 4 33.3% | 12 100% |
| Total | 55 19.3% | 46 16.1% | 72 25.3% | 62 21.8% | 50 17.5% | 285 100% |

Table 125: Chi-Square test done when comparing education level against "To share photos or videos" preference.

| | Value | Degree of freedom (df) | Assumption |
|---|---|---|---|
| Pearson Chi-Square | 13.435 | 12 | .338 |
| Likelihood Ratio | 15.131 | 12 | .234 |
| Linear-by-Linear Association | .725 | 1 | .395 |
| No. of valid Cases | 285 | | |

72

Table 126:" To communicate with friends out of the country" preference is compared to Education level.

| Education level | To communicate with friends out of the country | | | | | |
|---|---|---|---|---|---|---|
| | 1 | 2 | 3 | 4 | 5 | Total |
| Secondary School | 26 | 16 | 12 | 6 | 10 | 70 |
| | 37.1% | 22.9% | 17.1% | 8.6% | 14.3% | 100% |
| Post-Secondary | 44 | 19 | 29 | 12 | 19 | 123 |
| | 35.8% | 15.4% | 23.6% | 9.8% | 15.4% | 100% |
| Tertiary Level | 20 | 9 | 10 | 8 | 7 | 54 |
| | 37.0% | 16.7% | 18.5% | 14.8% | 13.0% | 100% |
| Vocational | 1 | 1 | 2 | 3 | 3 | 10 |
| | 10.0% | 10.0% | 20.0% | 30.0% | 30.0% | 100% |
| Total | 91 | 45 | 53 | 29 | 39 | 257 |
| | 35.4% | 17.5% | 20.6% | 11.3% | 15.2% | 100% |

Table 127: Chi-Square test done to comparing education level against "To communicate with friends out of the country"

| | Value | Degree of freedom (df) | Assumption |
|---|---|---|---|
| Pearson Chi-Square | 10.840 | 12 | .543 |
| Likelihood Ratio | 10.251 | 12 | .594 |
| Linear-by-Linear Association | 2.419 | 1 | .120 |
| No. of valid Cases | 257 | | |

Table 128: Education level is compare against "To play games" preference.

| Education level | To play games | | | | | |
|---|---|---|---|---|---|---|
| | 1 | 2 | 3 | 4 | 5 | Total |
| Secondary School | 21 | 12 | 10 | 7 | 17 | 67 |
| | 31.3% | 17.9% | 14.9% | 10.4% | 25.4% | 100% |
| Post-Secondary | 49 | 12 | 13 | 5 | 11 | 90 |
| | 24.3% | 20.9% | 23.6% | 13.5% | 17.6% | 100% |
| Tertiary Level | 20 | 3 | 4 | 3 | 4 | 34 |
| | 58.8% | 8.8% | 11.8% | 8.8% | 11.8% | 100% |
| Vocational | 1 | 1 | 0 | 0 | 4 | 6 |
| | 16.7% | 16.7% | .0% | .0% | 66.7% | 100% |
| Total | 91 | 28 | 27 | 15 | 36 | 197 |
| | 46.2% | 14.2% | 13.7% | 7.6% | 18.3% | 100% |

Table 129: Chi-Square test done "To play games" preference against education level.

| | Value | Degree of freedom (df) | Assumption |
|---|---|---|---|
| Pearson Chi-Square | 23.128 | 12 | .027 |
| Likelihood Ratio | 22.072 | 12 | .037 |
| Linear-by-Linear Association | 1.646 | 1 | .199 |
| No. of valid Cases | 197 | | |

# Appendix A-3

## Survey Questioner

Dear Participant,

You are invited to participate in a web-based online survey on what motivation attracts different users to use Facebook. This is a research project being conducted by Deo Farrugia, a student at the University of Derby. It should take approximately 15 minutes to complete.

PARTICIPATION
Your participation in this survey is voluntary. You may refuse to take part in the research or exit the survey at any time without penalty. You are free to decline to answer any particular question you do not wish to answer for any reason.

BENEFITS
You will receive no direct benefits from participating in this research study. However, your responses may help us learn more about the use of Facebook.

CONFIDENTIALITY
Your survey answers will be sent to a link at esurv.org where data will be stored in a password protected electronic format. esurv.org does not collect identifying information such as your name, email address, or IP address. Therefore, your responses will remain anonymous. No one will be able to identify you or your answers, and no one will know whether or not you participated in the study.

WITHDRAWAL
Please note that, while you can withdraw your participation from the survey at any time, it will not be possible to withdraw your data once you have submitted the survey.

CONTACT
If you have questions at any time about the study or the procedures, you may contact my research supervisor, Dr Eleanor Dare via email at E.Dare@derby.ac.uk.
If you feel you have not been treated according to the descriptions in this form, or that your

rights as a participant in research have not been honoured during the course of this project, or you have any questions, concerns, or complaints that you wish to address to someone other than the investigator, you may contact the Senior Administrative Assistant – Quality Customer Support and Operations University of Derby Online Learning Room S204, Kedleston Road, Derby, DE22 1GB T: +44 (0)1332 591139

1. What is your age?

14-17
18-21
22-34
35+

2. What is your Gender?

Male
Female

3. Your education Level?

Primary School level
Secondary school level
Post-Secondary level
Vocational School (Trade school)
Tertiary Education Level

4. You're Facebook 'status' update?

Daily
Weekly
Monthly
Yearly
Never

5. How long have you been signed up on Facebook?

Weeks

Months

Years


6.  How often Update profile picture?

A few times a day

A few times a week

A few rimes a month

A few times a year

Never



7.  How many "Groups" have you joined on Facebook?

None

1-10

11-20

21 or more


8.  More than one Facebook account?

Yes

No



9.  What application you use on Facebook?

Games

Music

Videos


10. Do you use Facebook on different devices?

Yes

No

11. Do you prefer communicating with friends by....?

Facebook
Email
Skype
Phone

12. Type of friends you have on you Facebook account.

For the following statements, please state your agreement/disagreement by putting a sign on the box below 1-5, where 1 means strongly disagree, 5 means strongly agree.

|  | 1 | 2 | 3 | 4 | 5 |
|---|---|---|---|---|---|
| School Friends |  |  |  |  |  |
| Friends you actually never met |  |  |  |  |  |
| Family members |  |  |  |  |  |
| Old friends |  |  |  |  |  |
| Foreign Friends |  |  |  |  |  |

13. Who can see your profile?

Everyone
Friends of friends
Only friends

14. What do you typically use Facebook for?

For the following statements, please state your agreement/disagreement by putting a sign on the box below 1-5, where 1 means strongly disagree, 5 means strongly agree.

|  | 1 | 2 | 3 | 4 | 5 |
|---|---|---|---|---|---|
| To communicate with friends |  |  |  |  |  |
| To communicate with family members |  |  |  |  |  |
| To communicate with friends out of the country |  |  |  |  |  |
| Play games |  |  |  |  |  |
| Share photos or videos |  |  |  |  |  |

Thank You for participating in the Survey!
Your Survey has been successfully submitted.

Over the last few years social network websites have become a global phenomenon and brought great social impact across the world. Such happenings deserve to be studied and their many aspects investigated thoroughly. The aim of this study was to explore the motives and preferences of users on Facebook. The data was obtained through an online survey on 383 random participants. The result confirmed that Facebook has become a powerful medium of communication. (...)

**www.grin.com**

Document Nr. V298721
http://www.grin.com
ISBN 978-3-656-95073-8

9 783656 950738